Cambridge Elements

Elements in Complexity and Agent-Based Economics

ACTIVE PARTICLES METHODS IN ECONOMICS

New Perspectives in the Interaction between Mathematics and Economics

Nicola Bellomo
University of Granada

Diletta Burini
University of Perugia

Valeria Secchini
Charles University

Pietro Terna
University of Turin

Shaftesbury Road, Cambridge CB2 8EA, United Kingdom

One Liberty Plaza, 20th Floor, New York, NY 10006, USA

477 Williamstown Road, Port Melbourne, VIC 3207, Australia

314–321, 3rd Floor, Plot 3, Splendor Forum, Jasola District Centre, New Delhi – 110025, India

103 Penang Road, #05–06/07, Visioncrest Commercial, Singapore 238467

Cambridge University Press is part of Cambridge University Press & Assessment, a department of the University of Cambridge.

We share the University's mission to contribute to society through the pursuit of education, learning and research at the highest international levels of excellence.

www.cambridge.org
Information on this title: www.cambridge.org/9781009548748

DOI: 10.1017/9781009548755

When citing this work, please include a reference to the DOI 10.1017/9781009548755

First published 2024

A catalogue record for this publication is available from the British Library.

ISBN 978-1-009-54874-8 Hardback
ISBN 978-1-009-54876-2 Paperback
ISSN 2732-5067 (online)
ISSN 2732-5059 (print)

Active Particles Methods in Economics

New Perspectives in the Interaction between Mathematics and Economics

Elements in Complexity and Agent-Based Economics

DOI: 10.1017/9781009548755
First published online: November 2024

Nicola Bellomo
University of Granada
Diletta Burini
University of Perugia
Valeria Secchini
Charles University
Pietro Terna
University of Turin

Author for correspondence: Nicola Bellomo, nicola.bellomo@polito.it

Abstract: The aim of this Element is to understand how far mathematical theories based on active particles methods have been applied to describe the dynamics of complex systems in economics, and to look forward to further research perspectives in the interaction between mathematics and economics. The mathematical theory of active particles and the theory of behavioral swarms are selected for the above interaction. The mathematical approach considered in this work takes into account the complexity of living systems, which is a key feature of behavioral economics. The modeling and simulation of the dynamics of prices within a heterogeneous population is reviewed to show how mathematical tools can be used in real applications.

Keywords: economic modeling, interacting agents, active particle, price emergence, mathematical modelling

JEL classifications: C02, C60, C78

ISBNs: 9781009548748 (HB), 9781009548762 (PB), 9781009548755 (OC)
ISSNs: 2732-5067 (online), 2732-5059 (print)

Contents

1 Aims and Plan of the Element

Interactions between mathematics and economics have led to a number of successful scientific achievements, up to and including Nobel Prizes. For example, we refer to Nash (1951, 1996), for the 1994 award shared by Harsanyi, Nash, and Selten for their analysis of equilibria in the theory of non-cooperative games; and to Black and Scholes (1972, 1973), for the 1997 awards shared by Merton and Scholes for their Black–Merton–Scholes option pricing formula.

In some cases, interdisciplinary interactions have led to advances in both fields. For example, the celebrated theory of games and equilibria was developed by Nash, while the pricing model has led to interesting studies in the qualitative analysis of partial differential equations. On the other hand, the challenging goal of developing a mathematical theory of economics (at least for certain branches of economics) has not yet resulted in a well-defined and robust theory, although it has attracted intense attention from scientists working in both fields.

Recently, some progress has been made using methods inspired by methods from statistical physics, which initially attracted mathematicians to the modelling of immune competition, see Bellouquid and Delitala (2006), and on biological systems in general, see Aristov (2019). We refer to the book of Bellomo, Bellouquid, Gibelli, and Outada (2017), updated in the review of Bellomo et al. (2021), for the *kinetic theory of active particles*, KTAP for short, while various surveys, for example see Ajmone Marsan, Bellomo, and Gibelli (2016) and Dolfin, Leonida, and Outada (2017), report on specific applications to the modelling of a variety of living systems.

Somewhat technically different approaches have been developed in parallel to the KTAP. For example, see Pareschi and Toscani (2013), which presents mathematical tools partially inspired by methods of statistical physics, in particular the Boltzmann and Fokker–Plank equations, as well as the survey by Furioli, Pulvirenti, Terraneo, and Toscani (2017) devoted to modelling social systems and economics.

The KTAP approach has inspired various approaches that use analogous concepts but employ different mathematical structures. Indeed, this is the case with the *theory of behavioural swarms*, TBS for short, which is based on mathematical structures inspired by pseudo-Newtonian dynamics, namely systems of ordinary differential equations. This theory was proposed in Bellomo, Ha, and Outada (2020) and has already been applied to modelling and simulation of systems in economics. In particular, it has already been specialized for the modelling of price dynamics in Bellomo, De Nigris, Knopoff, Morini, and Terna (2020) and Knopoff, Secchini, and Terna (2020).

It is not surprising that mathematicians, motivated by problems in economics, look to the methods of statistical physics. Studies in economics are well aware of this tendency – for instance, see Jovanovic and Le Gall (2021) – as well as of the useful contributions that can be made by the mathematical theory of dynamical systems already applied within deterministic frameworks; see Bonacich and Lu (2012).

The purpose of our Element is to understand how far mathematical theories based on active particles methods have been applied to describe the dynamics of complex systems in economics, and to look forward to further research perspectives in the interaction between mathematics and economics. Indeed, we live in a complex behavioural, and evolutionary environment, as observed in the collection of essays edited in Ball (2012), which reports on a variety of applications.

We are aware that this research program cannot be developed on the basis of mathematical approaches generally applied to inert matter. Therefore, the search for new methods should go far beyond the current state of the art. In fact, it requires the invention of new mathematical tools, even a new mathematical theory, capable of capturing, as far as possible, the main features of living systems. There exists a critical literature on the conceptual difficulties concerning the interaction between mathematics and living systems in general; see May (2004) and Reed (2004). This difficulty is caused by the lack of background field theories that are otherwise available in the case of living systems. Furthermore, living systems are evolutionary; see Mayr (1981). A reference for the philosophical and mathematical rationale for overcoming these difficulties can be found in Burini, Chouhad, and Bellomo (2023).

In our Element, we take into account this specific indication and address the study to a large system of several interacting living entities. We refer mainly to the TBS approach. However, we also consider the conceptual genesis of TBS from the KTAP approach. The presentation is mainly conceptual, but bibliographical references are given to support the interest of readers in mathematical topics. The content of our Element is presented in the following sections and an appendix devoted to scientific programming.

Section 2 presents a general strategy for modelling systems of living interacting entities. The strategy leads to the derivation of a mathematical structure suitable for capturing the key complexity features of living systems. Reference to the existing literature indicates that the concept of living systems should also be extended to behavioural sciences such as economics and political science. Therefore, this section provides an introduction to the contents of the following sections devoted to the search for mathematical tools in economics.

Section 3 is devoted to the presentation of mathematical tools. First, we provide a brief overview of the approach of the *kinetic theory of active particles*, then we move on to the so-called *behavioural swarms theory*, see Bellomo, Ha, and Outada (2020). The conceptual difference between these two methods is that the state of each individual entity in swarms is defined by a deterministic variable, which, however, is statistically distributed among the interacting individuals, while in the case of the kinetic theory methods it is approximated by a probability distribution over the variable that defines the state of the micro-scale of the entities that make up the whole system.
Section 4 shows how the tools reviewed in Section 3 can be applied to the modelling and simulation of evolutionary and behavioural systems. The focus is on the dynamics of prices in a heterogeneous society, which is selected as an example. First, the derivation of the model is presented, and then the predictive ability of the model is examined by means of various simulations. This application is critically analysed in the following section with an eye towards further conceivable developments of the modelling approach.
Section 5 develops a critical analysis of the two methods and provides some hints for further technical and research developments. In particular, we consider the problem of modelling individual and collective learning dynamics, as this dynamics play a key role in several (possibly all) real-world applications involving living entities. Further topics considered in this section are modelling multi-model dynamics, exogenous networks and the use of the two previously mentioned methods in synergy. The development of new structures proposed in this section are motivated by specific applications which will be mentioned in the section itself.
Section 6 looks ahead to research perspectives along the quest to study the complex interactions between the hard sciences and life. This section also discusses how economics can be viewed as a behavioural science, taking into account some aspects typical of living systems. The final discussion focuses on the key objective of developing a mathematical theory of behavioural economics.
Section 7 provides the computational code for the simulations as a technical appendix. The scientific programs refer to the dynamical system presented in Section 4. The use of the codes is explained in detail so that the interested reader can use the codes for further computational studies. The codes can be technically extended to study different models. In particular, those derived within the formal framework of the kinetic theory of active particles with discrete states proposed in Section 5.
Section 8 proposes a conclusion to this Element with some considerations that start from the specifics of the soft and hard sciences and suggest a new vision

that goes beyond this division and focuses on the search for a mathematical theory of economics. It is hoped that the reader will find in this final section some pointers to perspectives.

2 On a Quest towards a Mathematical Theory of Living Systems

The content of this section is divided into three parts. First, we present some basic concepts about the derivation of mathematical (generally differential) models. Then, we propose some conceptual steps in the search for a mathematical theory of living systems. In particular, we show how these steps lead to a mathematical theory. Finally, we present a technical approach for deriving and validating specific models. These topics are covered in the following three subsections. Only concepts are given, as the subsequent mathematical formalization is provided in Section 3.

The content of the subsections aims at answering the following three key questions:

KQ1: ***What is a mathematical model?***
KQ2: ***What is the rationale for deriving mathematical models?***
KQ3: ***How can models be validated?***

2.1 On the Derivation of Mathematical Models

Our goal is to build a bridge between mathematics and economics. Therefore, for the purposes of the tutorial, we provide some technical definitions that are useful for a general methodological approach to modelling dynamical systems. Indeed, it is important to follow a general rationale instead of applying heuristic methods that may be valid in certain case studies, but cannot be easily applied to other case studies.

We refer specifically to a large system of interacting, *behavioural entities* that constitute a system in economics. We consider systems with a constant number of entities. Therefore, the overall state of the system can be provided according to the specific scale chosen for representing and/or modelling the system. In particular, one can consider the following scales and related classes of equations that provide the mathematical structure for deriving models.

Microscopic when the overall state is defined by the state of each individual entity, it can be called *active particle*, or *a-particle* for short. The state of the a-particles is called *activity*. Microscopic models are usually described by systems of ordinary differential equations.

Mesoscopic when the overall state is defined by a probability distribution over the state of the microscale entities that make up the system, called *active particles*. Mesoscopic scale models are generally described by systems of transport equations with the structure of integro-differential equations.

Macroscopic when the overall state is defined by the local mean and higher-order moments of the activity. Microscopic models are usually described by systems of partial differential equations.

This brief introduction naturally leads to an understanding of the general concept of the mathematical model. We focus on the lower scales, while the macroscale quantities are obtained by local averaging of the microscale activity. The following definitions are proposed for this purpose.

Independent and Dependent Variables: Independent variables are time and space, which are also defined independently of the system object of the modelling approach. *Dependent variables* are the quantities that depend on the time and space selected in the mathematical model to describe the overall state of the system. These variables are sometimes referred to as *state variables*. The state variable at the micro scale is defined by the set of all activities expressed by the a-particles, since the activity is heterogeneously distributed among the a-particles. At the mesoscale, the system is defined by a probability distribution over the microstate.

Definition of a Mathematical Model: A *mathematical model* is an equation or computer description suitable for describing the dynamics of a system. Models are generally referred to as *mathematical structures*, which are related to the scale chosen to represent and model the system.

Functional Subsystems and Endogenous Networks: A-particles can express different types of activities. Therefore, the whole system can be divided into different aggregations called *functional subsystems,* or FS for short. *Endogenous networks* correspond to a system of nodes, where each FS is localized in a node. The communication between the nodes, namely in the network, can take place through different communication devices, while spatial dynamics is not taken into account.

Exogenous Networks: Space collocation is considered in *exogenous networks*, where nodes correspond to a physical collocation. Each node consists of an endogenous network. Therefore, the two networks are subject to a complex dynamics of interactions.

All the preceding definitions naturally lead to the definition of mathematical models.

A mathematical model is a system of equations whose solution, given initial and boundary conditions, defines the dynamics of the system's state variable over the independent variable.

Remark 2.1 *As mentioned, we are considering systems with a constant number of a-particles. However, these can move through both types of lattices. The spatial dynamics does not appear, since it corresponds to the nodes of the exogenous lattice. In the following, we consider models derived in the framework of differential equations. In principle, the same simulation goal can be achieved by computer architecture.*

2.2 On a Quest towards Model of Living Systems

Behavioural systems in economics can be considered as a special class of systems belonging to the broader class of living systems. Therefore, a mathematical approach has been developed that takes this special feature into account, as first reported in Bellomo (2008) and later in Bellomo et al. (2017). These books refer to the *kinetic theory for active particles*.

Subsequently, a pseudo-Newtonian approach was proposed in Bellomo, Ha, and Outada (2020) to pursue the same goal. This approach has been called the *mathematical theory of behavioural swarms*.

The next section presents an overview and critical analysis of the two aforementioned methods, while here we simply report on the philosophy that gave rise to these methods. Actually, we refer to the reasoning given in Bellomo et al. (2017) for the first method and show how it provides the pseudo-Newtonian methods as well. The key point is that the search for a mathematical theory of living systems requires a strategy suitable to replace the background theories, consisting of conservation and/or equilibrium equations, which refer to systems of inert matter and which may include source/sink terms related to competition and dissipation/decay somehow related to entropy functions.

In fact, living systems are different. This was noted by **Immanuel Kant (1724–1804)**, who defined living systems as *special structures organized and with the ability to pursue a purpose* (Kant, 2000).

It may be noted that **Lee Hartwell (born 1939)**, Nobel Laureate, expressed an analogous concept: 'Although living systems obey the laws of physics and chemistry, the concept of function or purpose distinguishes biology from other sciences. In fact, cells are not molecules, but have living dynamics induced by the lower level of genes and are organized into organs' (Hartwell, Hopfield, Leibler, and Murray, 1999, p. 647).

This statement concerns the organizing capacity of cells to organize themselves into biological structures, which opens up the search for the complex connections between genes and cells, where the dynamics at the level of genes induce the dynamics at the level of cells. This multiscale vision applies not only to biology, but to all living systems in general, including the economy.

Furthermore, **Herbert A. Simon (1916–2001)** teaches us how behavioural features should be considered by economic systems, since several aspects of the dynamics of systems in economics are influenced by individual strategies generated by learning and the ability to express specific strategies up to decision making. These features, which are evolutionary in time, are heterogeneously distributed in the individual or aggregate active particles that play interactions (games) in economics; see Simon (1978, 2019). Simon, similar to Hartwell, states that formally structured theories are possible for economics and gives hints on how to pursue this goal. Such a theory should be developed within a multiscale vision in which the dynamics at all scales are constantly interacting.

It is not surprising that most of the search for a mathematical theory of living systems has been related to biology, as evidenced by some pioneering work; see Bellomo and Forni (1994), Bellouquid and Delitala (2006), and Jager and Segel (1992). These are examples where the preceding concepts have been used in different mathematical settings, but without the framework of a global strategy. More recently, however, research has focused on social systems and behavioural and evolutionary economics; see Ajmone Marsan et al. (2016) and Bellomo, Dosi, Knopoff, and Virgillito (2020).

Given the preceding brief introduction, we can now present the modelling strategy, which consists of two steps. First, we consider the derivation of a mathematical structure suitable to capture the complexity features of living systems. Then, the second step consists in deriving models by inserting into such a structure models of interactions for the specific system object of the modelling approach.

Step 1 is performed through the following sequence of blocks shown in Fig. 1:

- **Block 1** Phenomenological interpretation of living systems to extract the specific features of complexity, as well as the phenomenology of the dynamics of interactions at the micro-scale.
- **Block 2** Identification, from the study in Step 1, of the activity expressed by the *active particles*, and subdivision of the overall systems into groups of the same interest, already defined *functional subsystems*.

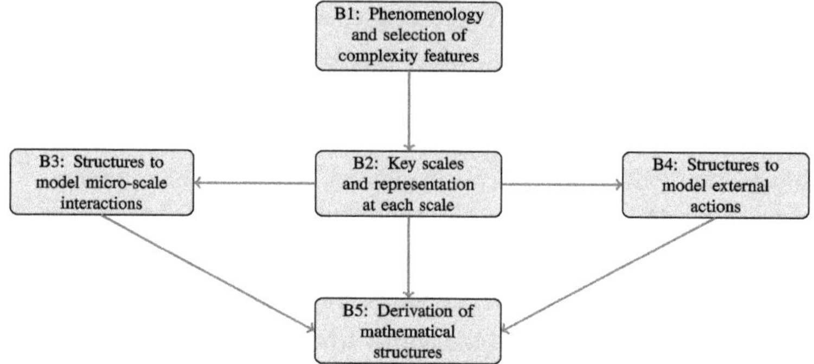

Figure 1 Strategy towards mathematical structures to model living systems.

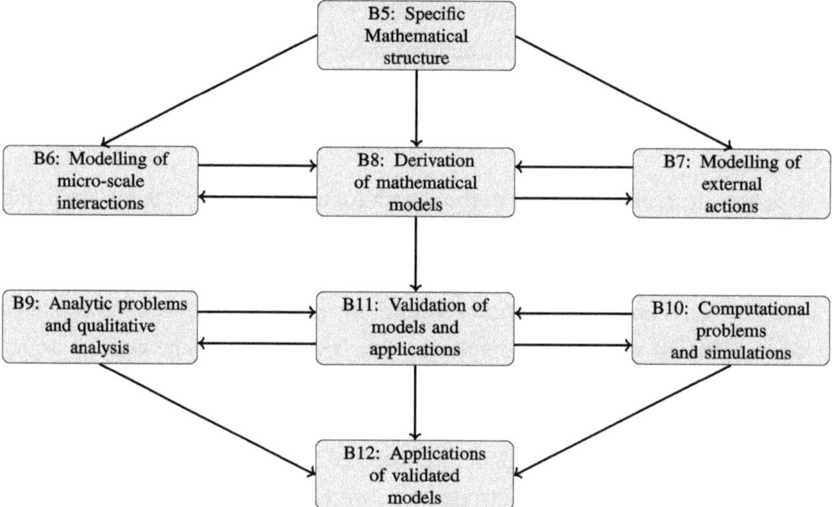

Figure 2 From mathematical structures to models and applications.

- **Block 3** Design of mathematical structures suitable for describing m-m and m-M interactions, where these abbreviations correspond, respectively, to interactions between microscopic entities and between microscopic and macroscopic entities.
- **Block 4** Design of mathematical structures suitable for describing the external actions acting on active particles and on the system as a whole.
- **Block 5** The derivation of a general mathematical structure capable of capturing the complexity features defined in Step 1, consistent with the chosen representation and modelling scale. This structure should transfer micro-scale interactions to the description of collective behaviour.

The approach is performed through the following sequence of blocks, shown in Fig. 2:

- **Step 1** Derivation of mathematical models (Block 8) by inserting into the mathematical structure (Block 5) the interactions between a-particles (Block 6) and the external actions acting on active particles and on the system as a whole (Block 7).
- **Step 2** Validation of models (Block 11) requires simulations (Block 9) and qualitative analytical studies (Block 10).
- **Step 3** Validated models can be applied to specific case studies using simulations and analytical results (Block 12).

Remark 2.2 *Interactions may be nonlinearly additive and nonlocal in space. An important feature is that the sensitivity of a-particles to other a-particles may not be symmetric. Models of interactions can be based on a phenomenological study of each specific system object of the modelling approach.*

Remark 2.3 *Models present a nonlinear structure that requires the development of computational codes that must be related to such specific structures. For example, behavioural swarms require the treatment of large systems of ordinary differential equations, while kinetic theory for active particles can be treated by Monte Carlo methods for the simulation of large systems of interacting particles.*

Remark 2.4 *The application of models to real-world problems can generate challenging analytical problems in addition to computational ones. A key problem is the study of the asymptotic trend time of the dynamical response, searching for the existence and stability of equilibrium configurations, when it is possible to prove their existence. Another challenging problem is the derivation of macroscopic models from the underlying description at the microscopic scale.*

A selection of the most important complexity features is necessary, since we cannot naively claim that all of them are effectively considered. Our proposal is based on the authors' bias in some way consistent with Bellomo et al. (2017). Accordingly, the following five common features and sources of complexity are selected.

- *Ability to express a strategy* is modeled by the *activity variable*, say *behavioural "soft" variable*, then all components can have a mutual influence. If the strategy contains both behavioural and mechanical variables, then the latter are influenced by the former.
- *Heterogeneity* can be modeled by a distribution function over the activity to account for the heterogeneous behaviour of a-particles, which can be viewed as probability distributions.

- *Nonlinearity of Interactions:* Modelling interactions generally leads to nonlinear additive outputs, which may also depend on the distribution functions. For example, models of opinion formation include the sensitivity of a-particles not only to individual a-particles, but also to individuals as a whole.
- *Learning Ability:* A-particles learn from past experience, as shown in Burini and De Lillo (2019) and Burini, De Lillo, and Gibelli (2016). As a consequence, the dynamics of the interaction are modified by the level of learning that is heterogeneously acquired by each individual. A key issue to be considered in modelling learning are the physics of the human mind, in Schoeller, Perlovsky, and Arseniev (2018), and the complexity of the cognitive process, in Perlovsky and Schoeller (2019).
- *Darwinian Mutation and Selection:* All living systems are evolutionary, as birth processes can produce entities that are either less or more adapted to the environment. The less adapted may even die out, while the more adapted may produce new entities that are better adapted to the external environment.

These complexity features, and additional possible ones, imply that the modelling approach always needs *multiscale methods*, where the dynamics at the large scale should be properly related to the dynamics at lower scales. For example, the behaviour of individual entities depends on their individual ability to develop strategies based on the amount of information stored in their minds due to past experience.

Collective behaviours are observed at the macroscopic scale, with the understanding that the dynamics of a few entities do not directly lead to the collective dynamics as already observed in Anderson (1972). In addition, the role of the external environment can have an important influence on the dynamics. Therefore, appropriate models and parameters are needed to account for this type of action. The interaction with the external environment can generate mutations and selections, which can lead to the strengthening or weakening of FSs.

2.3 On the Validation of Mathematical Models

Let us now consider the validation of models by examining their ability to quantitatively reproduce empirical data, if available. Furthermore, models are also required to represent, on a qualitative level, the observed emergent collective behaviour. This is not an easy task, as several technical difficulties have to be taken into account. These are related to the multiscale structure of the systems under consideration and to their properties as living systems. The validation process should take into account that different types of models can be derived according to the different types of predictive description they can offer. In particular, two main typologies of models can be identified:

- **Predictive models**, which aim to predict, qualitatively and quantitatively, the behaviour of systems in time, given appropriate initial conditions and, if necessary, constraints on the solutions. In addition, models should also reproduce qualitatively emerging behaviours that are often qualitatively repeated within appropriate variations of the parameters of any mathematical problem.
- **Exploratory models**, which aim at exploring the behaviour in time of systems under programmed variation of parameters and external actions. In fact, in the case of open systems, the role of external actions must be studied to verify whether or not these actions have the ability to address the system towards specific behaviours.

The validation of models generally encounters technical difficulties. For example:

1. Models are often derived at a scale different from that used to observe and collect empirical data. For example, interaction models refer to the microscopic scale, but collective behaviour is observed at the macroscopic scale.
2. Collective dynamics are subject to large deviations depending on the parameters that model the interactions as well as the initial conditions.
3. The amount of empirical data needed to develop a detailed validation process generally corresponds to steady uniform states, in some cases equilibrium, while models should describe dynamics far from such states.

Remark 2.5 *The key difficulty is then quantitative empirical data are generally available, but only for very special case; for example, small perturbations of steady states. Therefore, even when available these data may not be useful. On the other hand, we focus on collective behaviours which can be observed in several cases. Studying the ability of models to reproduce qualitatively observed collective behaviours is already a key contribution to validation. Indeed, validation can take advantage of the fact that qualitative forms of collective behaviours are preserved in most cases. One can call them "emerging behaviours."*

Models could hopefully demonstrate a very special case of emerging behaviour, which is the occurrence of unpredictable events with the characteristics of the so-called *black swan*, defined as follows according to Taleb (2007): "*A Black*

Swan is a highly improbable event with three principal characteristics: It is unpredictable; it carries a massive impact; and, after the fact, we concoct an explanation that makes it appear less random, and more predictable, than it was."

3 A Handbook of Mathematical Tools

This section shows how the rationale proposed in Section 2 can be translated into an analytic formalization, with the aim of providing a concise handbook of mathematical tools to be applied to modelling and simulation of systems in behavioural economics. We refer to the mathematical theory of active particles, which includes both the kinetic theory approach and the theory of behavioural swarms.

The common feature of these two methods is that the collective motion depends on the interactions at the microscopic scale. On the other hand, an important difference characterizes them. In fact, the KTAP approach refers to the conceptual lines of statistical physics, while the TBS refers to a pseudo-Newtonian framework. In fact, the information provided by KTAP is richer than that given by TBS, but the KTAP approach requires a sufficiently large number of a-particles to justify the statistical description, while this constraint is not necessary for the application of TBS methods.

Although the application reviewed and critically analyzed in the next section refers specifically to the TBS approach, both methods will be reviewed in this section, while a critical analysis will point out pros and cons of the two methods and will work out some developments towards a possible unification of the two methods.

We consider the dynamics of a finite number of a-particles. In the first subsection we review the kinetic theoretical approach, while in the second subsection the mathematical theory of behavioural swarms is reviewed. A critical study, focusing mainly on conceivable developments of the two methods, is reviewed in the third subsection.

Before giving additional details of these two theories, it would be useful to make precise the terminology about interactions, collisions, scattering, and games. The specific theories are somewhat inspired by the methods of the statistical physics of classical particles, where the term *interaction* is systematically used to denote the mutual action of two particles. This definition refers to a pair of particles that are *scattered* due to the interaction, but preserving mass, linear momentum, and energy. The scattering is related to the fact that the centers of the two particles do not coincide along their respective trajectories. The term *collision* is also used, although it is valid for billiard balls, but not always for particles that do not collide thanks to repulsive forces.

When we move to *active particles*, the term *collision* cannot be accepted and it is often replaced by *interaction*, although it seems generic because it does not express the strategy that modifies the rules of interaction. Often theoretical tools of game theory are used to model the outcome of the interaction. Then a-particles become players and interactions correspond to a game. Nevertheless, we often use the term *interactions* because game theory is not the only way to account for strategies and related outcomes.

3.1 On the Kinetic Theory of Active Particles

Let us consider the dynamics of a large system of a-particles, which can be divided into m FSs, denoted by the subscript i. The number N of a-particles is assumed to be constant in time, since we do not consider birth and death dynamics. However, a-particles can move across FSs. This overview of mathematical tools refers to Bellomo et al. (2017), reviewed also in Bellomo, Esfahanian, Secchini, and Terna (2022).

The state of the system is one whose state is defined by the distribution functions:

$$f_i = f_i(t, u) : [0, T] \times D_u \longrightarrow \mathbb{R}_+, \qquad i = 1, \ldots, m, \tag{3.1}$$

where D_u is the domain of activity u and T is the maximal observation time.

Remark 3.1 *The strategy expressed by individuals, namely a-particles, is heterogeneously distributed over the microstates of a-particles considered as players. These are modeled as stochastic variables associated with a distribution function over the microstates. The payoff is also heterogeneously distributed over the players and can be motivated by 'rational' but also 'irrational' strategies.*

If f_i is known and integrable, the low order moments provide the macroscopic state of the system. Specifically, the fraction of a-particles in each FS, with respect to N, is given by

$$n_i = n_i(t) = \int_{D_u} f_i(t, u)\, du, \tag{3.2}$$

where

$$\sum_{i=1}^{m} n_i(t) = 1, \tag{3.3}$$

since we have assumed that N is constant.

Similar calculations lead to the mean:

$$\mathbb{E}_i = \mathbb{E}_i(t) = \int_{D_u} u f_i(t,u)\, du, \tag{3.4}$$

and variance

$$\mathbb{V}_i = \mathbb{E}_i(t) = \int_{D_u} (u - \mathbb{E}_i)^2 f_i(t,u)\, du. \tag{3.5}$$

Of course, analogous calculations can be applied to the whole system.

Remark 3.2 *The activity is different in each FS, but the notation is simplified by writing u instead of u_i, since the subscript denotes both the FS and the activity. In general, dimensionless variables are used by referring the activity to the minimum and maximum values, say u_m and u_M, so that $D_u = [0,1]$ or $D_u = [-1,1]$ when it is useful to consider positive and negative values of the activity.*

The KTAP approach considers the following types of statistically identified a-particle:

- ***Test*** particle, which is supposed to be representative of the whole system, of the *i*th functional subsystem with microscopic state, at time t, supplied by the variable u, whose distribution function is $f_i = f_i(t,u)$.
- ***Field*** particle of the *k*th functional subsystem with microscopic state, at time t, defined by the variable u^*, whose distribution function is $f_k = f_k(t,u^*)$. By field particles we mean the complete set of particles.
- ***Candidate*** particles, of the *h*th functional subsystem, with microscopic state, at time t, defined by the variable u_*, whose distribution function is $f_h = f_h(t,u_*)$. Candidate particles are the field particles that end up in the test particle state after interaction.

Interactions modify the activity of a-particles, which can also move across FS. Each a-particle has a sensitivity range $\Omega \subseteq D_u$ and is therefore only sensitive to activity within Ω. Interactions may be non-symmetric. In this case the notation Ω_u is used to denote an activity dependent sensitivity. There are two kinds of interactions:

- ***Micro-micro interactions***, in short m-m, by which each a-particle interacts with other a-particles of all FSs whose state falls in Ω.
- ***Micro-macro interactions***, in short m-M, through which each a-particle interacts with all FSs identified by the mean value $\mathbb{E}$ whose state falls within Ω_u.

The modelling of the interactions can be supplied by the following quantities:

- ***m-m interaction rate*** $\eta_{ik}[f_i,f_k](u_*,u^*)$, which models the frequency of micro-micro interactions between a candidate i-particle with state u_* and a field k-particle with state u^*.
- ***m-M interaction rate*** $\mu_{ik}[f_i,f_k](u_*,\mathbb{E}_k)$, which models the frequency of micro-micro interactions between a candidate i particle with state u_* and the FS_k with macroscopic state given by the mean value of the activity $\mathbb{E}_k$.
- ***Transition probability density due to m-m interactions***, which models the probability density that a candidate i-particle with state u_*, after a micro-micro interaction with a field k particle of state u^*, is denoted by $\mathcal{A}_{ik}[f_h,f_k](u_* \to u|u_*,u^*)$.
- ***Transition probability density due to m-m interactions***, which models the probability density that a candidate i-particle with state u_* ends up in the state of the test particle of the ith FS after a micro-macro interaction with the k-FS, is denoted by $\mathcal{B}_{ik}[f_h,f_k](u_* \to u|u_*,\mathbb{E}_k)$.
- ***Loss terms due to m-m interactions***, which models the loss of the number of particles corresponding to micro-micro interactions described by $\mathcal{A}_{ik}$, is denoted by $\mathcal{L}_i[f_i,f_k](u,u^*)$.
- ***Loss terms due to m-M interactions***, which models the loss of number of particles corresponding to micro-micro and micro-macro interactions due to conservative interactions described by $\mathcal{B}_{ik}$, is denoted by $\mathcal{K}_{ik}[f_i,f_k](u,\mathbb{E}_k)$.

The derivation of the mathematical structures that provide the conceptual framework for the modelling is obtained by the number balance of a-particles within an elementary volume of the space of microscopic states of the active particles. More specifically, the rate of change of the number of active particles is equal to the input flux minus the output flux for both micro-micro and micro-macro interactions.

Balance within the space of microscopic states can be described as follows:

Variation rate of the number of active particles

= *Inlet flux rate caused by conservative interactions*

– *Outlet flux rate caused by conservative interactions*

+ *Inlet flux rate caused by proliferative interactions*

– *Outlet flux rate caused by destructive interactions,* (3.6)

where all the proceeding fluxes include both micro-micro and micro-macro interactions, as well as the dynamics of mutations.

If only conservative interactions are taken into account, the preceding relation corresponds to the following structure:

$$\frac{\partial}{\partial_t} f_i(t,u) = \big(\mathcal{G}_i - \mathcal{L}_i + \mathcal{H}_i - \mathcal{K}_i\big)[f_h,f_k](t,u), \tag{3.7}$$

where

$$\mathcal{G}_i = \sum_{k=1}^{n} \int_{\Omega_u \times \Omega_u} \eta_{ik}[f_i,f_k](u_*, u^*) \mathcal{A}_{ik}[f_i,f_k]\,(u_* \to u|u_*, u^*) \times f_i(t,u_*) f_k(t,u^*)\, du_* du^*, \tag{3.8}$$

$$\mathcal{L}_i = f_i(t,u) \sum_{k=1}^{n} \int_{\Omega_u} \eta_{ik}[f_i,f_k](u,u^*) f_k(t,u^*)\, du^*, \tag{3.9}$$

$$\mathcal{H}_i = \sum_{k=1}^{n} \int_{\Omega_u} \mu_{hk}[f_i,f_k](u_*, \mathbb{E}_k(t)) \mathcal{B}_{ik}[f_i,f_k]\,(u_* \to u|u_*, u^*) \times f_i(t,u_*) \mathbb{E}_k(t)\, du_*, \tag{3.10}$$

and

$$\mathcal{K}_i = f_i(t,u) \sum_{k=1}^{n} \mu_{ik}[f_i,f_k](u, \mathbb{E}_k(t)). \tag{3.11}$$

Let us now consider the modelling of interactions, where different models of interactions are reported in the following examples:

Competitive (Dissenting): One of the interacting a-particles increases its status by taking advantage of the other, which is forced to decrease its status. Competition brings advantage to only one of them.

Cooperative (Consensus): The interacting a-particles exchange their states, namely the a-particles with higher states decrease their states, while the others with lower states increase their states. All a-particles show a tendency to share their microstate.

Learning: One of the two a-particles changes its microstate independently of the other. It learns by reducing the distance between the activities of the interaction particles. The distance in measured by an appropriate metric technically related to the specific dynamics under consideration.

Hiding: One of the two tries to increase the total distance from the other, which in turn tries to decrease it.

Mixed competitive-cooperative: A-particles do not share the same strategy, but some of them act competitively while others act cooperatively.

Remark 3.3 *The payoff that leads to the decision depends on the actions of the players as well as the frequency of interactions. Both may depend on the overall probability state of the system.*

Remark 3.4 *A technical generalization of the structures is the use of vector activity variables, which requires modelling a hierarchy of the components of* *the activity variable so that the transition probabilities can be factorized. This problem is tackled by the kinetic approach, where the modelling of interactions is described by theoretical tools of stochastic game theory. This approach deals with entire populations of players, where strategies with higher payoff could spread over each population through learning related to individual-based and collective interactions, where the concept of learning has been defined earlier.*

Remark 3.5 *The mathematical structures reported in this subsection have been derived under the assumption that interactions, although behavioural, follow rules that are constant in time. A recent study is inspired by Herbert Simon's theory of the virtual world; see Simon (2019). In detail, the mathematical framework proposed in Bellomo and Egidi (2024) models a dynamics whose interactions evolve in time. The driver of this action is the* ***Utility Function*** *which evolves in time consistently with the overall dynamics of the system.*

The preceding mathematical tools have been reported for a dynamics with constant number of particles. This assumption is consistent with the specific models of economics studied according the KTAP approach. On the other hand, the theory is more general and includes a variable number of individuals due to proliferative and/or destructive events. Therefore, the preceding structures need further developments that are reported in the following with the aim of providing a more general framework consistent with Eq. (3.6). The assumption that the previously mentioned event occur in the state of i-particles leads to the following balance of particles:

$$\partial_t f_i(t,\boldsymbol{u}) = \left(\mathcal{C}_i - \mathcal{L}_i + \mathcal{M}_i^M - \mathcal{L}_i^M + \mathcal{P}_i - \mathcal{D}_i + \mathcal{P}_i^M - \mathcal{D}_i^M\right)[f_i,f_k](t,\boldsymbol{u}). \quad (3.12)$$

If we only consider proliferative and destructive terms that are generated by interactions at the micro-scale, the following additional terms are considered:

$$\mathcal{P}_i = \sum_{k=1}^{n} \int_{\Omega\times\Omega} \eta_{hk}[f_i,f_k](\boldsymbol{u}_*,\boldsymbol{u}^*)\mathcal{P}_{ik}[f_i,f_k](\boldsymbol{u},\boldsymbol{u}^*) \times f_i(t,\boldsymbol{u}) f_k(t,\boldsymbol{u}^*)\, d\boldsymbol{u}^*, \quad (3.13)$$

and

$$\mathcal{D}_i = f_i(t,\boldsymbol{u}) \sum_{k=1}^{n} \int_{\Omega} \eta_{ik}[f_i,f_k](\boldsymbol{u},\boldsymbol{u}^*)\, \mathcal{D}_{ik}(\boldsymbol{u},f_k) f_k(t,\boldsymbol{u}^*)\, d\boldsymbol{u}^*, \quad (3.14)$$

with the meaning of the terms $\mathcal{P}_{ik}$ and $\mathcal{D}_{ik}$ analogous to that of the conservative terms.

- ***Transition probability density due to m-m interactions***, which models the probability density that a candidate i-particle with state u_*, after a micro-micro interaction with a field k particle of state u^*, is denoted by $\mathcal{A}_{ik}[f_h,f_k](u_* \to u|u_*,u^*)$.

- ***Transition probability density due to m-m interactions***, which models the probability density that a candidate i-particle with state u_*, after a micro-micro interaction with a field k particle of state u^*, is denoted by $\mathcal{A}_{ik}[f_h,f_k](u_* \to u|u_*,u^*)$.

The formal expressions of $\mathcal{P}_i^M$ and $\mathcal{D}_i^M$ is not reported here, as they can be obtained by analogous calculations.

The preceding mathematical structures do not consider transitions from one functional subsystem to the other. However, some specific models might require the modelling of this specific feature. Examples can be found in political dynamics, where individual entities might move from one political orientation to another. This topic is postponed to Section 5, where it is revisited considering both methods, that is, KTAP and behavioural swarms, including their synergetic applications in specific case studies.

3.2 Mathematical Tools of Behavioural Swarms

The so-called *theory of behavioural swarms*, or TBS for short, was introduced in Bellomo, Ha, and Outada (2020) and subsequently applied to modelling and simulation of problems in economics, which will be reviewed in what follows. As in the case of the kinetic theory of active particles, the TBS approach refers to a mechanical system. Specifically, this theory is based on the Cucker–Smale model; see Cucker and Smale (2007), which describes the dynamics of a fixed number of self-propelled particles. This model is therefore a pioneering description of the dynamics of animal swarms.

It is useful to write the model because it helped to clarify the conceptual developments that lead to a new class of models that can be of interest in economics as well as in other fields of science related to the study of living systems. Let us consider an ensemble of mechanical Cucker–Smale particles whose states are represented by position and velocity variables. More precisely, let $\boldsymbol{x}_i$ and $\boldsymbol{v}_i$ be the position and velocity of the ith C-S particle, respectively, in the free Euclidean space $\mathbb{R}^d$. Then the time evolution of the mechanical variables $(\boldsymbol{x}_i, \boldsymbol{v}_i)$ is governed by the Newton-like system:

$$\begin{cases} \dfrac{d\boldsymbol{x}_i}{dt} = \boldsymbol{v}_i, \quad t > 0, \quad 1 \le i \le N, \\ \dfrac{d\boldsymbol{v}_i}{dt} = \dfrac{\kappa}{N} \displaystyle\sum_{j=1}^{N} \phi(\|\boldsymbol{x}_j - \boldsymbol{x}_i\|) \left(\boldsymbol{v}_j - \boldsymbol{v}_i\right), \end{cases} \tag{3.15}$$

where $\|\cdot\|$ denotes the standard ℓ^2-norm in $\mathbb{R}^d$, κ represents the strength of coupling, and the communication weight $\phi\colon [0,\infty) \to \mathbb{R}_+$ is bounded, Lipschitz continuous, and monotonically decreasing.

Let us now review the mathematical tools necessary to apply the theory. First, we define the interacting entities, their aggregation, and the rules of interaction that lead to the mathematical framework of TBS theory.

General System: We consider a system N of interacting living entities, all with the structure of an a-particle whose state is activity. We consider systems where space and speed variables do not modify the dynamics which is homogeneous in space. The mathematical structures underlying the derivation of the models can be derived within a *pseudo-Newtonian framework*, where for each a-particle, the action of the other a-particles produces an acceleration for the activity variable.

Active Particles and Functional Subsystems The individual entities, i.e., *a-particles*, are carriers of a behavioural state, called *activity*, which defines their *microstate*. Active particles can be grouped into m *functional subsystems*, often referred to by the acronym j-FS, with $j = 1, \ldots, m$. Each individual a-particle, that is, ij-particle, is labeled by the subscripts i, where $i = 1, \ldots, n_j$, and j, identifying each i-particle and each j-FS, respectively.

Microstate of a-Particles The state of each a-particle is a scalar denoted by the variable $u \in D_u$, which corresponds to the activity of the ij particles. In general, the range is $D_u = [-1, 1]$. More generally, the activity can be a vector.

Interactions, as in the case of the KTAP approach, can be both micro-micro and micro-macro. In general, interactions are nonlocal and nonlinearly additive. A key property of ij particles is the sensitivity domain $\Omega_{ij} \subseteq D_u$ within the space of the activity variable. The ij particle perceives the presence of all hk particles whose microstate lies within Ω_{ij}. The functions that model the interactions are the following:

- $\eta_{ij}^{hk} = \eta_{ij}^{hk}\left(u_{ij}, u_{hk} | u_{hk} \in \Omega_{ij}\right)$ models the *interaction rate* of micro-scale interactions between the ij-particle with all hk-particles in Ω_{ij}.
- μ_{ij}^k models the *micro-macro interaction* of the individual-based interactions between the ij-particle and the k-FS as a whole, which can be the mean value of the activity $\mathbb{E}_k$. Then, $\mu_{ij}^k = \mu_{ij}^k(u_{ij}, \mathbb{E}_k)$.
- $\varphi_{ij}^{hk} = \varphi_{ij}^{hk}\left(u_{ij}, u_{hk} | u_{hk} \in \Omega_{ij}\right)$ models the *micro-scale action* occurring at the rate η_{ij}^{hk}, applied by all hk particles in Ω_{ij} to the activity variable of the ij particle.
- $\psi_{ij}^k = \psi_{ij}^k(u_{ij}, \mathbb{E}_k)$ models the *micro-scale action* that occurs at rate μ_{ij}^k on the activity variable over the ij particle by each j FS.

These definitions lead to the ***mathematical structures*** by connecting cause and effect, namely actions on the a-particles, with pseudo-accelerations. In detail, u_{ij} is the activity of the ij particle and v_{ij} is its velocity, defined as the time derivative of u_{ij}. Then the mathematical structure modelling the dynamics of these dependent variables is a second-order system consistent with a pseudo-Newtonian framework:

$$\frac{d^2 u_{ij}}{dt^2} = \sum_{h=1}^{n}\sum_{k=1}^{m} \eta_{ij}^{hk}\left(u_{ij}, u_{hk} | u_{hk} \in \Omega_{ij}\right)\, \varphi_{ij}(u_{ij}, u_{hk}) + \sum_{k=1}^{m} \mu_{ij}^{k}\left(u_{ij}, \mathbb{E}_k\right)\, \psi_{ij}^{k}\left(u_{ij}, \mathbb{E}_k\right). \tag{3.16}$$

Remark 3.6 *The sensitivity domain is assumed to coincide with the entire domain of the activity variable, for example* $D_u = [-1, 1]$. *Interactions can be non-symmetric, for instance,* $\Omega = [-a, b]$ *for positive defined constants such that* $a \leq 1$ *and* $b \leq 1$. *If* $a < 1$ *and/or* $b < 1$, *the information does not sufficiently support the decisional process.*

The mathematical tools reviewed in this subsection refer to a pseudo-Newtonian framework. The system is nonlinear as interactions are, as mentioned, nonlinearly additive. The book by Wei-Bin Zhang presents a review and critical analysis, specifically focused on economics, based on Newton-type methods that go far beyond application of Lotka–Volterra methods economics; see Zhang (2023). This book shows also how a qualitative and computational study of systems in economics can provide useful information on the predictive ability of models.

3.3 Critical Analysis towards Unified Theories

The two mathematical methods discussed in this section have been derived according to the same principles, but presenting substantial differences. In addition to those we have already presented, we will propose some considerations that can lead to new structures closer to each other in the spirit of the unification of physical-mathematical theories proposed in the Hilbert's sixth problem; see Hilbert (1902). The considerations in this subsection are presented on a qualitative level, since their formalization in a mathematical framework should, in our opinion, be treated for each specific case study.

The approach of the kinetic theory requires that the specific systems under consideration consist of a sufficiently large number of active particles, while the theory of behavioural swarms requires a sufficiently small number, not only to avoid excessive computation, but also to have the possibility of identifying each particle individually. Actually, this is not important when the state of all particles is the same, but it may become necessary when it is heterogeneously distributed. However, these considerations are too vague to be used as a quantitative criterion. In particular, if you say *large* and *small* in reference to the number of a-particles, these adjectives are not quantitatively defined.

Of course, computational approximation methods can deal with this difficulty. For example, agent methods or differential systems with random initial conditions can be used. However, it is worth exploring further development of the kinetic theory approach to make it somewhat consistent with the behavioural properties of each specific system under consideration.

One method worth considering is the use of discrete values to represent the probability distribution. In fact, this approach is not simply an approximation device, but can be viewed as an interpretation of the model based on the assumption that particles whose state is confined to a small domain behave according to the same rules. This approach was used in Bellomo, Dosi, et al. (2020), resulting in a mathematical tool that preserves the descriptive power of kinetic theory, for example the ability to describe transitions across FSs, and captures the specificity of the mathematical theory of behavioural swarms.

All topics mentioned in this subsection, as mentioned earlier, will be considered and revisited in Section 5. In fact, applications demand a unified vision of the two approaches. Therefore some further developments are necessary in both methods also, as their contextual use is, in some specific case-studies, useful. In this framework, it is important that modelling of interactions follow the same rules. The following list indicates the most important features that should be shared in both approaches. Theoretical tools of game theory can contribute to model them.

- *Stochastic game theory deals with entire population of players, where strategies with higher payoff might spread over the population.*
- *The strategy expressed by individuals, namely, active particles, is heterogeneously distributed over players.*
- *Players are modeled as random variables linked to a distribution function over the activity variable.*
- *The pay-off is heterogeneously distributed over players and it can be motivated by "rational" or even "irrational" strategies.*
- *The payoff depends on the actions of the coplayers as well as on the frequencies of interactions. Both quantities depend on the overall state of the system.*
- *In the virtual world the payoff is substituted by the so-calld Utility Function.*

These interactions generate nonlinearities in the structure used for modelling. Let us consider the mathematical structures of the KTAP approach presented in Subsection 3.1. These are nonlinear due to the product of the dependent variables f_i. This is a *quadratic nonlinearity* analogous to that of the nonlinear Boltzmann-type models. If the terms modelling interactions, namely $\eta, \mu, \mathcal{C}, \mathcal{M}, \mathcal{P}, \mathcal{D}, \ldots$, do not depend on $[f_h, f_k]$, but only on the activity variable, interactions are defined as *linear*. On the other hand, when these terms depend on $[f_h, f_k]$, the interactions are defined as *nonlinear*. In this case, the mathematical structure presents a double type of nonlinearities and occasionally the term *multiple nonlinearity* is used.

The same considerations can be addressed to the dynamics of swarms, but in this case the micro-state variables are the dependent variables. Therefore, nonlinearity is referred directly to these variables.

If interactions within the domain Ω are considered, it is useful to understand more about symmetries of interactions. Then, if a-particles are sensitive with respect to u, uniformly in Ω, interactions are *symmetric*, and otherwise are *non-symmetric*. This considerations can be referred to both types of mathematical structures.

4 On Price Dynamics in Heterogeneous Societies

This section shows how the mathematical tools reviewed in Section 3 can be applied to modelling behavioural economics; see Bellomo, Dosi, et al. (2020), where individual behaviours are heterogeneously distributed in a population that can be divided into functional subsystems. The application discussed in this section is related to the conceptual framework of the mathematical theory of behavioural swarms. However, before dealing with this specific application, it is useful to have a brief look at the various applications to modelling and simulation in economics, based on the methods reviewed in our Element. This overview is presented in the next subsection, while the remaining two subsections deal with modelling and simulating the dynamics of prices in a heterogeneous population.

In fact, the idea of developing methods from the hard sciences for behavioural economics can be found in the visionary book by Herbert Simon (2019). The first edition of this book was published in 1996. This edition did not immediately attract the attention of mathematicians, but today it is an important reference in the quest towards the development of mathematical tools to describe the dynamics of systems of behavioural economics. Other important readings are cited here, also with tutorial purposes, Schumpeter (1947); Stiglitz (2010).

4.1 A Brief Review of Applications of Active Particles Methods

The kinetic theory of active particles, as reported in the recent survey Burini et al. (2023) and book Bellomo et al. (2017), was first developed to model the competition between cancer cells and the immune system, then further developments focused on modelling social dynamics such as opinion formation; see Bertotti and Delitala (2004, 2010). These papers were soon followed by studies on the dynamics of economic interactions with social and political dynamics: Bertotti (2010), Bertotti and Modanese (2011), Dolfin, Knopoff, Leonida, and Patti (2017), Dolfin and Lachowicz (2014, 2015), and Dolfin, Leonida, and Outada (2017).

The idea of linking social dynamics and economics is somewhat consistent with the guiding philosophy of behavioural economics; see Thaler (2016) and Thaler and Sunstein (2009). Then the applications moved to evolutionary economics, Dolfin, Knopoff, et al. (2017); see Dosi (1984), Dosi, Fanti, and Virgillito (2020), Dosi, Pereira, and Virgillito (2017), and Dosi and Virgillito (2021). This literature has also been reviewed in Bellomo et al. (2022), which is a useful reference for this Element. The recently published book provides an excellent overview of the foundation of evolving economics; see Dosi (2023).

Turning now to the kinetic theory of active particles, we note that this quest for a mathematical theory of living systems has a long history. Indeed, the idea of developing kinetic theory models in which the microstate includes an internal behavioural state was first developed in seminal papers in which this concept was introduced. We refer specifically to Jager and Segel (1992), which focused on modelling the social dynamics of certain populations of insects, where interactions led to the splitting of the populations into dominant and dominated; and to the modelling of evolutionary immune competition between tumor and immune cells from Bellomo and Forni (1994) to Bellouquid and Delitala (2006).

The scientific literature on swarms has been arguably initiated by physicists, while the interest of mathematicians was stimulated by the visionary, so-called Cucker–Smale model, see Cucker and Smale (2007). Specific models can be derived for particles carrying a social variable, such as a social or political opinion; an analogous structure has been used to study and control the dynamics of the collective behaviour of one or more populations; see Furioli et al. (2017). A key feature of the dynamics is to understand how internal variables, which we have called activity, evolve over time due to interactions and modify the collective behaviour of the system; see Bellomo, Ha, and Outada (2020).

The idea of modifying the Cucker–Smale model to describe the dynamics of financial markets has been proposed in Bellomo, De Nigris, et al. (2020), while a first step in applying the theory of behavioural swarms to economics is in Bellomo, De Nigris, et al. (2020), where activity is modeled to reproduce a perfectly competitive market with decentralized prices and elementary processes of price adaptation through swarm dynamics. However, the mathematical theory of behavioural swarms is quite recent and needs further development.

Therefore, further applications are expected once dynamics such as mutation and selection are introduced into the theory. These are necessary ingredients to derive models of evolutionary biological systems. However, evolutionary systems present common features and we argue that applications of the theory in economics will also consider this specific feature.

4.2 Buyers and Sellers and Price Dynamics

An application, consistent with the guidelines of our Element, focused on the modelling of price dynamics is proposed in Knopoff et al. (2020) by a further development and enrichment of the so-called cherry picking dynamics. In this approach, the price quality is an important factor in the collective dynamics. In particular, this paper develops an earlier approach to this problem in Bellomo, De Nigris, et al. (2020).

We borrow the general description of the model from the open access paper Knopoff et al. (2020). This allows us to provide a description of the assumptions that lead to the derivation of the model without repeating all the analytical details that lead to the differential systems in Eqs. (7) and (9) in Knopoff et al. (2020), which define the mathematical models.

In detail, consider a market in which N sellers and M buyers trade a given good, where both numbers are fixed. Sellers and buyers can be considered as functional subsystems. Within each FS, particles (i.e., sellers or buyers) express a heterogeneous activity. The activity variables for sellers and buyers are as follows:

- u_s, $s = 1, \dots, N$ corresponds to the first functional subsystem (sellers), where each s-firm expresses the price u_s of the product (good) offered for sale. The activity variable is the *price assigned by each seller*.
- w_b, $b = 1, \dots, M$ corresponds the second functional subsystem (buyers), where each b-buyer expresses the price w_b that he/she accepts to pay. The activity variable is the *price that each buyer accepts to pay* for the good.
- v_s, $s = 1, \dots, N$ and z_s, $s = 1, \dots, M$ denote the speed of the variables u and w.

Remark 4.1 *Both prices and related speeds are normalized with respect to their highest value at initial time $t = 0$; we can assume that $\boldsymbol{u}_0, \boldsymbol{v}_0 \in [0,1]^N$ and $\boldsymbol{w}_0, \boldsymbol{z}_0 \in [0,1]^M$. The dynamics can, however, generate values which do not belong to these intervals for larger times.*

The knowledge of micro-scale variables leads to macro-scale quantities such as the m-order moments within each FS:

$$\mathbb{E}_s^m = \frac{1}{N}\sum_{s=1}^{N} u_s^m \quad \text{and} \quad \mathbb{E}_b^m = \frac{1}{M}\sum_{b=1}^{M} u_b^m. \tag{4.1}$$

The assumptions underlying the derivation of the model are as follows:

- *Micro-micro interactions take place only between FSs, not within the same FS. In these interactions, firms and customers adjust prices through direct contact. Macro-micro interactions take place within the same FS, but not between different FSs. Through these interactions, each seller adjusts its price according to the average flow of sellers, while customers adjust the price according to the average flow of buyers.*
- *At each interaction, each buyer interacts with the seller having the lowest u_s among those offering at least the reservation quality of the buyer. The chosen seller has the lowest u_s among those offering at least the reservation quality of the buyer. The exchange takes place if $w_b \geq u_s$ at the price of u_s. If so, the buyer's reservation price w_b tends to decrease while the seller's price u_s tends to increase.*
- *The opposite happens when the exchange does not take place (when the buyer does not accept the seller's offered price because $w_b < u_s$). The term "tends to" is used to account for the change after the interaction does not act directly on the price, but on its velocity, because the model is based on a second-order system through swarm dynamics.*
- *In micro-micro interactions (described earlier), each agent adjusts its price by learning from past experience if its price (or reservation price) is too high or too low to sell or buy in the market, and changes it accordingly.*
- *At each macro interaction, each seller interacts with the other sellers as a whole, comparing its price with the first-order moment of its FS's prices (the average seller's price) and trying to move it closer to it. Again, through the information extrapolated by the micro-macro interactions, the seller learns and adapts its a-variable.*

The general structure which provides the conceptual framework towards the derivation of models is as follows:

$$\begin{cases} \dfrac{du_s}{dt} = v_s, \\ \dfrac{dw_b}{dt} = z_b, \\ \dfrac{dv_s}{dt} = \dfrac{1}{M}\displaystyle\sum_{q=1}^{M} \eta_s^q(u_s, w_q)\, \varphi_s^q(u_s, w_q, v_s, z_q) \\ \qquad\qquad + \mu_s(u_s, \mathbb{E}_s)\, \psi_s(u_s, \mathbb{E}_s), \\ \dfrac{dz_b}{dt} = \dfrac{1}{N}\displaystyle\sum_{q=1}^{N} \eta_b^q(w_b, u_q)\, \varphi_b^q(w_b, u_q, z_b, v_q) \\ \qquad\qquad + \mu_b(w_b, \mathbb{E}_b)\, \psi_b(u_b, \mathbb{E}_b), \end{cases} \tag{4.2}$$

for $s = 1, \ldots N$ and $b = 1, \ldots, M$.

Models are obtained by inserting into Eq. (4.2) a detailed modelling of the interactions, which are described by the following quantities:

- $\eta_s^b(u_s, w_b)$ models the rate at which a seller s interacts with a buyer b;
- $\eta_b^s(w_b, u_s)$ models the rate at which a buyer b interacts with a seller s;
- $\mu_s(u_s, \mathbb{E}_s)$ models the micro-macro interaction rate between a seller s and her/his own FS;
- $\mu_b(w_b, \mathbb{E}_b)$ models the micro-macro interaction rate between a buyer b and her/his own FS;
- $\varphi_s^b(u_s, w_b, v_s, z_b)$ denotes the micro-micro action, which occurs with rate η_s^b, of a buyer b over a seller s;
- $\varphi_b^s(w_b, u_s, z_b, v_s)$ denotes the micro-micro action, which occurs with rate η_b^s, of a seller s over a buyer b;
- $\psi_s(u_s, \mathbb{E}_s)$ denotes the micro-macro action, which occurs with rate μ_s of the FS of sellers over a seller s;
- $\psi_b(w_b, \mathbb{E}_b)$ denotes the micro-macro action, which occurs with rate μ_b of the FS of buyers over a buyer b.

As mentioned earlier, further details can be found in Knopoff et al. (2020). Here we conclude the presentation of the models with a few remarks that can guide the development of simulations.

Remark 4.2 *The system presents asymmetries, since the sellers' prices are public (*e.g., *advertised price tags), while the buyers' prices are unknown to the sellers. This feature is taken into account to properly model the interaction terms.*

Remark 4.3 *The system has a pseudo-inertia and it defines the time dynamics of the following quantities: the seller's price* u_s*, namely the price set by the seller for his product, and the buyer's reservation price* w_b*, namely the maximum price the buyer is willing to pay.*

Remark 4.4 *The elementary processes of price adjustment are based on the so-called Hayekian idea of a decentralized market. Hayek's idea is that the dynamics at the micro level are the cause of the dynamics at the macro level. This is also why the theory of the decentralized market has been used as a theoretical framework to construct models of price dynamics in agent-based models, such as in Mazzoli, Morini, and Terna (2019).*

4.3 Some Key Simulations

The model includes several parameters, among which the most important are the *quality of the seller's product* and the *quality of the buyer's reservation,* which is the minimum quality the buyer is willing to accept for the offered product. Also to be explained is the *Pareto market efficiency*: this quantity gives us a measure of the buyer's 'gain'. More specifically, it measures the difference between the maximum price the buyer was willing to spend and what he actually spent during the exchange with the seller.

The simulations developed in Knopoff et al. (2020) have shown the following characteristics of the dynamic description of the system:

1. When we reduce the interaction among sellers (we reduce the adjustment of sellers' prices based on other sellers' prices), buyers' prices begin to coordinate and divide into functional subsystems. The reduced interaction among sellers is necessary for buyers to express collective behaviour. Buyers divide themselves based on their reservation quality (buyers with the same reservation quality end up in the same clusters).
2. The coordination of buyers can occur in different numbers of clusters (from one to five), depending on the random initial conditions. This means that the formation of clusters is an endogenous effect. From an economic point of view, if allowed to do so, buyers manage to coordinate and create their preferred markets or the ones that are most convenient for them.
3. In the classical framework, goods with quality differences generate multiple markets. From this perspective, it is impossible to analyze buyers' behaviour in the face of quality differences. By considering micro-transactions with prices disclosed by the sellers (so-called adhesion contracts), we can instead study the effects of consumer control over quality on the market.

4. This buyer control of the market can also be seen in the study of *Pareto market efficiency*. When buyers manage to coordinate and be part of their most convenient market, we can observe a higher market efficiency compared to the case in which the collective behaviour is not achieved. This means that when sellers create some kind of "agreement" about their prices (in the model, when they have a high interaction among them), buyers suffer from a disadvantage.

The following simulations have been developed using the same parameters as the ones in the figures showing collective behaviour in Knopoff et al. (2020). Specifically, in these simulations, the parameter determining the seller-sellers interaction is lowered by one order with respect to the case in which the clustering does not appear. We can observe the evolution of buyers' prices and their division into functional subsystems depending on their reservation quality, identified by different colors, right before and during coordination, in the short and long run.

In detail, we observe the emergent capability of the agents to act in a coordinate way, showing the same reaction to price changes and so creating close groups (clusters). In Fig. 3 we can see the prices before they are fully divided and coordinated. In Fig. 4 we have a general and long-term view of the prices and we can see clusters divided by quality. A closer look at the prices once they are coordinated can be seen in Figs. 5 and 6 (in the latter we can observe a rare five-cluster coordination, in a closer look).

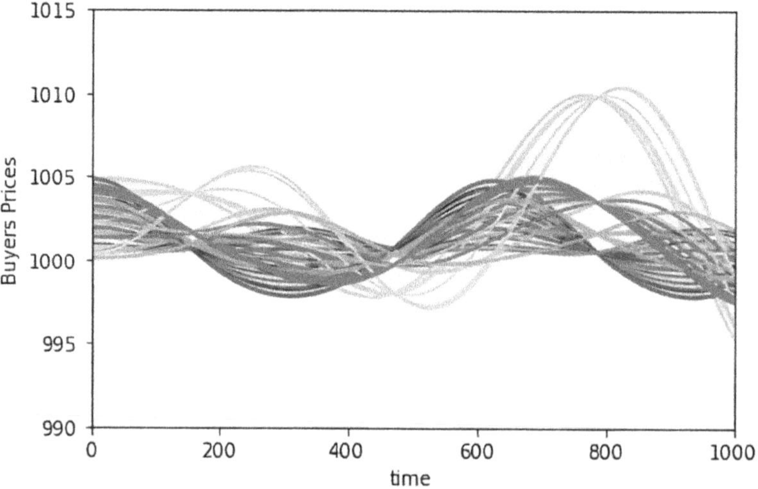

Figure 3 Buyers' prices: before coordination, view on the short run.

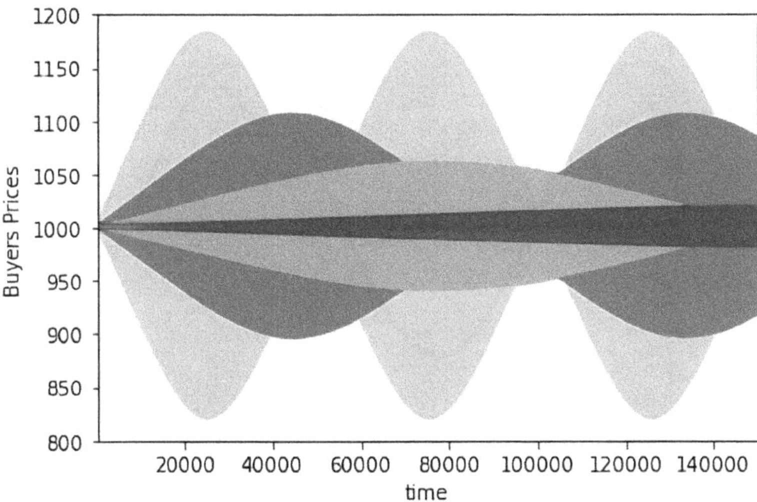

Figure 4 Buyers' prices: coordination and emergence of four clusters. Whole view of the long run.

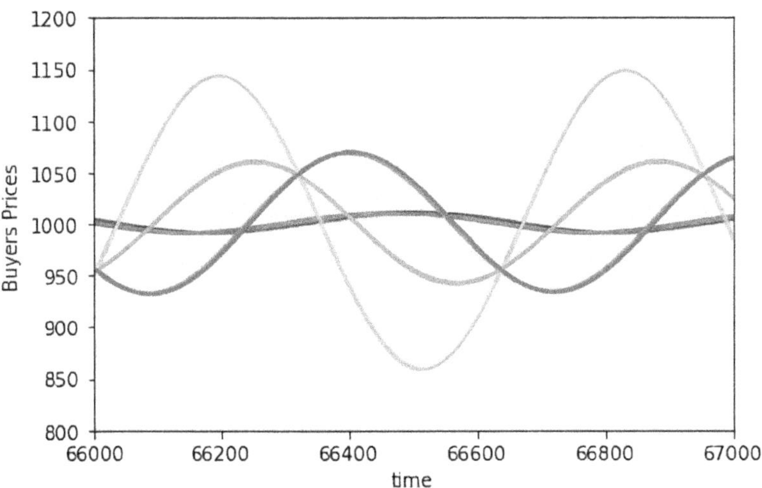

Figure 5 Buyers' prices: coordination and emergence of four clusters. Closer look on the long run.

5 Further Developments of Mathematical Theory

Two mathematical approaches have been presented in the previous sections. These methods correspond to two different scales and representations. Specifically, the kinetic theory model corresponds to the mesoscopic scale, while the swarm mode corresponds to the microscopic, individual-based scale. At each scale, two mathematical structures have been derived that lead to models that can be used either alternatively or synergistically.

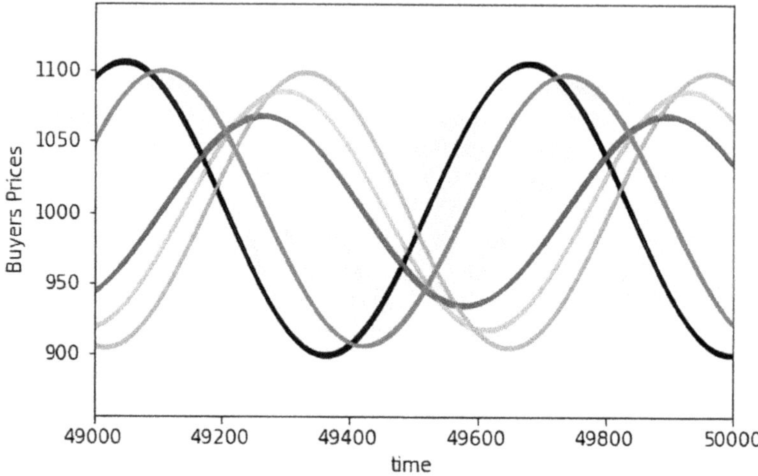

Figure 6 Buyers' prices: coordination and emergence of five clusters. Closer look on the long run.

This section develops an additional study of these two approaches to understand how each can be used in modelling real-world case studies. We also consider that economic systems generally cannot be observed and interpreted as stand-alone systems. For example, the dynamic in the economy is somewhat influenced by politics, which affects the management of the system, and could also be influenced by the population.

More generally, one should consider the action of politics, we mean governments, on systems in areas different from that of the system under consideration, but which can have an influence on the said system. Three examples can be given to materialize the preceding concepts.

Welfare policies that can generate support or opposition to governments. The study developed in Bellomo, Herrero, and Tosin (2013) shows how the collective tendency of citizens moves against a government that imposes an unfair wealth distribution. This opposition involves not only the poor classes that are harmed by unfair management, but also the wealthy classes that may be attracted by the average level of opposition, in addition to their own ethical sentiments.

The study of the interaction between lawbreakers and detectives was developed in the paper by Bellomo, Colasuonno, Knopoff, and Soler (2015), which shows that inequalities in the distribution of wealth increase the transfer of citizens to crime. This paper also shows that the effectiveness of detectives' actions improves more by acting on their training than by increasing their number.

These considerations provide evidence that collective learning is present in all the dynamics that appear in this case study.

The study of the interactions between economics and epidemics has been motivated by the recent pandemics of SARS-CoV-2. It is a challenging topic, as the recent literature has developed new multiscale methods to model the diffusion of epidemics by the approach of the kinetic theory of active particles. An interesting contribution has been made by Aguiar, Dosi, Knopoff, and Virgillito (2021), who also consider the role of communicating networks. Learning dynamics appear both in the communication between individuals in a population and in the immune competition at the scale of cells; see Burini and Knopoff (2024, in press).

In addition to the preceding examples, we can observe that the dynamics of the prices considered in Section 4, involves two groups of interest (we have called them functional subsystems). The numerical size of the two groups is very different, since the number of sellers is, in most cases, of a lower order with respect to the number of buyers. Therefore, we could consider using the theory of behavioural swarms for the sellers and the kinetic theory of active particles for the buyers.

These examples can help us to identify some key problems that deserve attention:

(i) Developing new mathematical tools from the current state of the art;
(ii) Understanding the physics of collective learning and the role of this specific dynamics in economics;
(iii) Deriving models for dynamics on networks and for multi-model systems.

These topics are covered in the next three subsections. We do not claim that the preceding list is complete. On the other hand, we hope that the contents of the following subsections can also contribute to the last section, where a critical analysis is proposed to understand how far we are from the derivation of mathematical economic theory.

The presentation focuses mainly on concepts rather than mathematical tools. In fact, this section looks ahead to perspectives where the concepts here should be transferred to appropriate connections between economics and mathematics.

5.1 Extensions of the Mathematical Theories

An important objective of the research activity in this field consists in exploring the common features of the two approaches and in designing new mathematical structures suitable to make technically possible the passage from one type of mathematical method to the other. In this specific case, the transition is from the microscopic to the mesoscopic scale.

We start from the consideration that the assumption of a continuous distribution function requires that the number of a-particles is sufficiently large to justify the continuity assumption of the distribution function. This difficulty can be overcome by mathematical structures with discrete states.

The first approach to this goal is to consider a structure for number-conserving interactions:

$$f_{ij} = f_{ij}(t; u_j); \quad i = 1, \ldots n; \quad j = 1, \ldots m, \quad \boldsymbol{f} = \{f_{ij}\}, \tag{5.1}$$

where the a-particle belonging to the ith functional subsystem with state u_j is denoted as ij-particle whose state is denoted by f_{ij}, while the state of the a-particle is given by $\boldsymbol{f} = \{f_{ij}\}$

A general mathematical structure suitable for dealing with systems that undergo only conservative interactions was proposed by Bertotti and Delitala (2004) and applied to modeling the distribution of wealth within a population of individuals who compete to increase their wealth but are also forced, through tax systems, to transfer some wealth from high to low levels of wealth. Their mathematical structure considered only binary interaction. The structure is as follows:

$$\frac{d}{dt} f_{ij} = \sum_{h=1}^{n} \sum_{q,k=1}^{m} \eta_{iq}^{hk} \mathcal{A}_{iq}^{hk}(q \to j) f_{iq} f_{hk} - f_{ij} \sum_{h=1}^{n} \sum_{k=1}^{m} \eta_{ij}^{hk} f_{hk}, \tag{5.2}$$

where:

η_{iq}^{hk} models the interaction rate for encounters between an iq-particle and a hk-particle.

$\mathcal{A}_{iq}^{hk}(q \to j)$ models the probability of transition of the iq-particle to the state of the ij-particle due to encounters with hk-particle.

Technical calculation can lead to a more general structure, where a-particles can move across functional subsystems. In addition the encounter rate and the transition probability can depend on $\boldsymbol{f}$. This structure is as follows:

$$\frac{d}{dt} f_{ij} = \sum_{p,h=1}^{n} \sum_{q,k=1}^{m} \eta_{pq}^{hk}[\boldsymbol{f}]\, \mathcal{A}_{pq}^{hk}(p \to i, q \to j) f_{pq} f_{hk} - f_{ij} \sum_{h=1}^{n} \sum_{k=1}^{m} \eta_{ij}^{hk}[\boldsymbol{f}] f_{hk}, \tag{5.3}$$

where:

η_{pq}^{hk} models the interaction rate for encounters between an pq-particle and an hk-particle.

$\mathcal{A}_{oq}^{hk}(p \to i, q \to j)$ models the probability of transition of the pq-particle to the state of the ij-particle due to encounters with hk-particles.

Remark 5.1 *The mathematical frameworks in Eqs. (5.2) and (5.3) can be further developed to include nonconservative interaction and the effect of each functional subsystem as a whole. However, this generalization is only a matter of technical calculations which can be made following the guidelines of the derivation presented in Section 3. Therefore, these calculations will not be repeated here.*

Remark 5.2 *The mathematical structures corresponding to behavioural swarms have not been studied exhaustively. Nevertheless, further developments seem technically possible to bring the theory to a descriptive capability as rich as that of the kinetic theory of active particles approach. In this case, the contextual use of the two methods will be effectively at hand.*

5.2 Dynamics of the Collective Learning

As mentioned earlier, learning dynamics is almost always present in the various dynamics that can be studied by the mathematical tools presented in this Element. In fact, the strategy developed by a-particles starts from an interpretation of the dynamics of the system through a collective learning process that supports decision making, which depends on the amount and quality of information acquired by the a-particles.

It is a collective learning that involves people who correspond to the a-particles of a functional subsystem or, in some cases, leaders who are carriers of a high level of knowledge that they transfer to the people. In this case we have two functional subsystems. An example that becomes more and more frequent in our society is that of interaction of *influencers* and *followers*. Therefore, it is useful in this Element first to define the main characteristics of this specific dynamic and, subsequently, how recent studies have approached this topic consistent with the conceptual framework of this Element. We refer to Bandura (1989) and Salomon and Perkins (1998) for the following definitions:

- Collective learning is generally defined as *a social process of cumulative knowledge, based on a set of shared rules and procedures that allow individuals to coordinate their actions in search for problem solutions.*

- **It is a cumulative dynamical process:** *as it accumulates over time*. In the learning dynamic both a term of growth and a term of loss come into play, but the former is greater than the latter.
- **Interactive**, *as the knowledge is transferred between agents through an interactive process*.
- **Individual/cognitive**, *which occurs in the mind of the individual as a social and participatory process*.
- **Social learning**, *which occurs when the individual learns new behaviours and concepts from others*. Social learning is often combined with other dynamics.

Collective learning dynamics are qualitatively different in each specific case study. However, it is important to develop a general modelling methodology that can be specialized for each case study. This type of study has been developed by Burini et al. (2016), with further specialization by Burini, Gibelli, and Outada (2017) for the study of modeling teaching in high school classrooms.

The study by the approach of the kinetic theory of active particles. The sequential steps of the approach are as follows:

1. **Perception:** Each individual possesses a perception domain within which the presence of other individuals is perceived with different intensities that depend, for instance, on the 'distance'.
2. **Interactions and Learning:** Interactions induce a learning process in which individuals modify (increase) their level of knowledge.
3. **Micro-Macro Interactions:** Each individual also learns from the collectivity viewed as a whole.

Remark 5.3 *Collective learning is the precursor of many, if not all, dynamics in social dynamics and economics. The open problem is to specialize the general approach to specific case studies in economics. As an example, we consider again the previously mentioned learning of detectives of the localization of lawbreakers and of the latter of the hunting by detectives. The induced strategy, which is in opposition for each functional subsystem, starts from the learning dynamics mentioned earlier.*

5.3 Multi-model Systems and Networks

As we have seen earlier, different types of dynamics generally interact in the systems under consideration. In particular, learning dynamics interact with security problems, wealth distributions, and others. Therefore, it is important that the methods reported in this Element are addressed to modeling the dialogue between functional subsystems with the aim of transferring the information appropriate for the specific dynamics object of the modeling approach. Then the dialog involves *influencers* and *followers*. As a perspective, the modelling of price dynamics proposed in Section 4 could be reconsidered in accordance with the preceding considerations.

Some of the previously mentioned considerations can be applied to exogenous networks with specific focus on the interaction among nodes. Social dynamics in exogenous networks have been treated by Knopoff (2014); see also Aguiar et al. (2021). A development of these studies is that the output of interactions should also include the previously mentioned division into *influencers* and *followers* by a specialization of the nodes into dominant and dominated.

The literature reviewed in this section shows that the methods presented in our Element refer to an interdisciplinary environment, where economics interact with other scientific areas. The reader interested in these interactions can find out about them in the following website:

www.modelingnature.org/training

A program of seven open access lectures for PhD students and young researchers

Title: *Collective Dynamics in Science and Society*;
Lecturers: *Nicola Bellomo, Diletta Burini, Giovanni Dosi, Livio Gibelli, Damian A. Knopoff, Pietro Terna, Nisrine Outada, Maria E. Virgillito.*

6 On a Forward Look to Research Challenges

The goal of this Element has been to build a bridge between mathematics and economics, with a special focus on behavioral economics. We have presented two mathematical methods, both somewhat inspired by statistical physics, and a mathematics for living systems. The previous sections have shown that and how the bridge has been built and that it has already led to some encouraging results. We can look forward to methodological perspectives and new applications to be pursued in an interdisciplinary framework.

We first proposed a philosophy and then showed how the theoretical concepts could be transferred into a mathematical framework. Of course, the philosophy retains the authors' point of view and reasoning, but in the context of the theory of the artificial world and bounded rationality. Now we will take the liberty of giving a limited space to our bias. Accordingly, three specific arguments will be selected from among several possible ones and brought to the attention of the reader. Then, the final remark refers to the reasoning of the authors from the perspective of a mathematical theory of economics.

This section proposes a critical analysis followed by a philosophical study of the content of this Element in view of the research activity that can be developed in the field. Specifically, towards a mathematical theory of behavioural economics. The quest is in three sequential steps.

1. Reflections on the interactions between the hard sciences and the social and economic sciences.
2. A historical overview of the development of the mathematical tools of statistical physics toward a mathematics of living systems.
3. Key points for a mathematical theory of behavioural economics.

These issues are addressed in the following subsections. We do not claim to have dealt exhaustively with the challenging objectives just mentioned, but we humbly assert that this Element can contribute with perspective ideas and hints at the difficult quest we are working on.

6.1 Hard Sciences and Social-Economical Sciences

As we have seen in Sections 1 and 2, we first proposed a philosophy to build the previously mentioned bridge and then showed how the theoretical concepts could be transferred into a mathematical framework. Of course, the philosophy retains the authors' point of view and reasoning, but in the context of the theory of the artificial world and bounded rationality. Now we will take the liberty of giving a limited space to our bias. Accordingly, three specific arguments will be selected from among several possible ones and brought to the attention of the reader. Then, the final remark refers to the reasoning of the authors from the perspective of a mathematical theory of economics.

1. ***The main difference between classical and active kinetic theory:*** *Classical kinetic theory and active particles methods share some common features, but they have significant differences. The main difference is that the interactions in the Boltzmann equation are binary, local, and reversible, whereas in the case of active particles, the interactions are nonreversible and local. In addition, the interactions can also be non-symmetric and generally involve more particles as we will see in the next subsection.*
2. ***What about the theory of behavioural swarms?*** *The properties of active particles also apply to behavioural swarms. Therefore, although the formal aspects of the structure are analogous, the interactions are completely different, and it is necessary to use new concepts such as pseudo-velocity and pseudo-acceleration. Again, the action on a particle is neither binary nor local.*

3. ***On the connection between microscopic and macroscopic description:*** *This issue has already been raised in Section 2 with respect to model validation. In fact, the two methods discussed in this Element provide a description at the microscopic scale, either through the statistical description of kinetic theory or through the individual-based picture provided by behavioural swarm methods. On the other hand, empirical data are generally observed at the macroscopic level. Then, the derivation of macroscopic models from the underlying description at the microscopic scale in the spirit of Hilbert's sixth problem, see Hilbert (1902), is motivated by the need of interpretation of empirical data toward validation of models. Some recent results have been proposed in the case of multicellular systems; see Burini and Chouhad (2022, 2023). An interesting perspective consists in extending these results to the case of behavioural agents.*
4. ***What about parallel approaches and possible developments?*** *The two methods discussed in this Element are not exhaustive of the mathematical tools that have been developed recently. Indeed, agent methods should also be considered; see Mazzoli et al. (2019) in economics, and Galam (2012) in the study of social systems. For an excellent excursus on the development of methods from statistical physics toward applications to the study of social systems, see Helbing (2010). Closer to the kinetic theory of active particles is the Boltzmann–Fokker–Plank approach developed in Pareschi and Toscani (2013). Rather than comparing all methods, we propose, as a challenging perspective, their development into a unified mathematical theory.*
5. ***Artifacts towards a new vision of mathematical economics:*** *We have learned from Herbert Simon the theory of artifacts and the virtual world. Applying this theory to the mathematical tools discussed in this Element means providing a mathematical description of interactions with rules that evolve over time and are modified by the interacting entities; see Bellomo and Egidi (2024). This means going far beyond deterministic population dynamics toward a unified mathematical theory.*

These considerations indicate that for both mathematical approaches, kinetic theory and swarm methods, the first step is the modelling of interactions, where the modelling should be guided by the interpretation of what living systems are. This is not an easy task, as we can learn from Celand (2019), since we should understand the physical essence of what living systems are. A possible interpretation is given in Section 2 concerning the search for the main complexity features that characterize them. The last point of the preceding list indicates that interaction rules evolve in time following the evolution of the artificial world in which the specific system is localized.

The modelling approaches are similar, but we have shown in the previous sections that the two methods transfer low-scale dynamics to collective motion in different ways. At present, we can say that the kinetic theory method is complete with respect to the swarm approach, since it takes into account the specific features of interactions mentioned in the first point. Interactions also take into account post-Darwinian mutations and selections related to competition through proliferative and destructive encounters. The mathematical theory of behavioural swarms can account for heterogeneity of interacting entities, multiple interactions, and various types of nonlinearities. However, further studies are needed to complete this theory.

6.2 On the Development of Mathematical Tools

The previous subsection has indicated that the mathematical tools of generalized kinetic theory are currently the most convincing approach to a complete mathematical theory of behavioural systems in general. Therefore, it may be interesting to present a brief historical reconstruction of how the method developed from some pioneering papers to very recent results.

1. Ilia Prigogine, Nobel Laureate, proposed a mathematical theory of vehicular traffic on highways based on the development of Boltzmann-like methods; see Prigogine and Herman (1971). The state of the system is described by a one-particle distribution function over the individual states of the driver-vehicle subsystem.
   Paveri-Fontana (1975) shows how interactions should be modeled by heterogeneous rules and introduces a probability description of the desired velocity distributed over the system. The modelling of interactions takes this specific distribution into account.
2. Jager and Segel (1992) propose a generalized Fokker–Plank model to describe the social behaviour of certain populations. The dynamics is that interactions divide the population into dominant and dominated.
3. Bellomo and Forni (1994) developed a kinetic theory approach that includes progression and competition between tumor and immune cells. The ideas proposed in this paper have been developed by various authors. The book by Bellouquid and Delitala (2006) presents a unified vision of the in-host competition. The competition ends either with the prevalence of tumor cells or with the successful defense of the immune system.
4. Some mathematicians rapidly understood that an analogy of biological dynamics with some behaviours of living systems could lead to the development of a mathematical theory of living systems. Then, several interesting

scientific papers appeared in the literature, see Bertotti and Delitala (2004, 2010) and Bertotti and Modanese (2011), as examples of a rich literature developed in this century.

5. The validity of kinetic theory for the modelling of the behavioural dynamics in different real-world systems has suggested to provide a formal presentation of the mathematical tools. This activity is documented in Bellomo (2008) for a modelling approach of Boltzmann-like models, and in Pareschi and Toscani (2013), mainly focused on specific features of Boltzmann–Fokker–Plank models.

While the mathematical theories based on binary interactions appeared, some applications in different fields, such as vehicular traffic, see Coscia, Delitala, and Frasca (2007), showed the need to model interactions, where the output is described by nonlinear maps with multiple interactions, where the utility functions could even depend on the distribution functions, that is, on the dependent variable of the models. Other applications have shown how the mathematical approach could model post-Darwinian mutations and selections; see Bellomo and Carbonaro (2011). Both dynamics should be considered in various fields of economics as documented in Dosi (2023).

Accordingly, applications in economics have been developed; see, for example, the study of the blockage between economic development and political competition, Dolfin, Knopoff, et al. (2017), and the study of the role of nonlinear interactions in altruism and selfishness in welfare dynamics, Dolfin and Lachowicz (2014). A comprehensive review of the literature in this area is provided by the review papers Ajmone Marsan et al. (2016) and Dolfin, Leonida, and Outada (2017). The role of networks is also considered; see Dolfin and Lachowicz (2014) and Knopoff (2014). This research motivated the mathematical theory formalized in Bellomo et al. (2017).

The final step on this path is the mathematical interpretation of the dynamics within the artificial world of Herbert A. Simon. The recent contribution in Bellomo and Egidi (2024) takes into account Simon's philosophy, which teaches that not only do interactions exhibit nonlinearities, but that the rules of interaction evolve over time due to the dynamics of the artificial world in which the interactions take place. Some seminal considerations can already be found in Kant (2000). The translation of Simons' theory into a mathematical framework has opened up a new and challenging line of research that is definitely worth developing. The main contribution in Bellomo and Egidi (2024) is a mathematical theory that describes how the interaction rules follow the utility function that evolves over time in the artificial world.

6.3 Towards a Mathematical Theory of Behavioural Economics

Let us now return to the remark made at the very beginning of this Element about the idea of moving beyond mathematical models to a mathematical theory. The first difficulty is that systems in economics are in several cases behavioural. Then, they are carriers of most of the complexity features of living systems. The difficulty of mathematical approaches to describing the dynamics of living systems has been demonstrated by eminent scientists. For example, Robert May notes that the study of living systems cannot rely on background theories such as those that produced the physical-mathematical theories of inert matter; see May (2004) and Reed (2004). Moreover, living systems are evolutionary, as we learn from Mayr (1981).

However, this Element has shown that the current state of the art has led to mathematical structures that can capture the key features of living systems. These structures provide a framework that merits the definition of a *mathematical theory*. It would then be useful to understand how this theory can be specialized into a mathematical theory in economics, similar to the methods that have been brought to the different branches of mathematical physics. We do not have an exhaustive answer to this challenging problem. Therefore, we simply offer the reader some preliminary considerations.

1. Selection of a specific branch of economics specialized by specific features that support the theory. For instance, behavioural, evolutionary, and so on.
2. Emphasis on modelling interactions, taking into account nonlinear additivity, evolution of interaction rules, micro-micro and micro-macro features of interaction rules.
3. Implementation of models of interactions into the general mathematical structures and then proceeding to the validation of models.

This process can be interpreted as a rational approach to derive mathematical models that goes beyond the heuristic derivation of phenomenological approaches. In fact, it refers to the rationale reported in Fig. 2. The new concept is that the derivation is based on well-defined mathematical structures.

> ***A deeper development of the second step of the preceding sequence might shift from a phenomenological approach to a mathematical theory.***

We do believe that this challenging perspective is worth being pursued according to the idea that new mathematical tools have to be invented in economics rather than using tools that are valid for inert matter. Indeed, the second step is the key passage to the derivation of the mathematical theory. We have seen that both mathematical approaches are based on the idea of a mathematical transfer of the dynamics at the microscopic scale to the collective dynamics of the whole system. Then, we can argue that the mathematical tools of the kinetic theory of active particles and those of behavioural swarms can effectively provide to the said tool. Therefore, the key problem is the modelling of the interactions.

New inventions are needed to provide significant progress in this topic. For instance, by understanding that the dynamics of interaction follow rules that are modified by the individuals playing the game and by the the external actions that have a strategy to modify them. As mentioned earlier, these rules evolve over time.

As we have seen, we have different tools suitable to transfer the dynamics at the micro-scale into collective dynamics. Hence, the key problem is the modelling of interactions. Bearing all the preceding in mind, let us define some important features of interactions whose rules evolve in time.

- *Interactions can be modelled by theoretical tools of game theory, which should consider entire populations of players, where strategies with higher payoff might spread over the population.*
- *The strategy expressed by individuals, namely active particles, in the interactions is heterogeneously distributed over the players of the population.*
- *Players are modeled as random variables linked to a distribution function over the activity variable.*
- *The Utility Function guides the output of interactions. It is heterogeneously distributed over players and can be motivated by "rational" or even "irrational" strategies. In some cases, interactions are asymmetric; see Lachowicz, Matusik, and Topolski (2024).*
- *In the virtual world the Utility Function depends also on the actions of the coplayers as well as on the frequencies of interactions. Both quantities depend on the overall state of the system.*

The overview proposed in our Element, has shown that the path to a mathematical theory in economics has been traced. It is a challenging path; however, it is worth trying also as some achievements by the kinetic theory approach have been effectively obtained. But what about using swarm theories? Some studies have been recently developed by using mathematical tools borrowed by the physical-mathematical theory of swarms; see Ha, Kim, Park, and Zhang (2019), Bae, Cho, Lee, Yoo, and Yun (2019), and Bae, Cho, Kim, and Yun (2019).

What about developments? Let us start from the books by Zhang (1991, 2023), who developed a mathematical theory of economics within the framework of the mathematical theory of ordinary differential equations and of the interpretation of the dynamics of real systems by causality principles. These models provide an immediate description of the dynamics and, at least in some cases, allow a qualitative analysis focused on asymptotic behaviours, stability, and bifurcation. An analogous approach is developed in Bonacich and Lu (2012), where a variety of specific applications are considered.

On the other hand, these methods fail in describing some specific features of real systems from the individual heterogeneity to all behavioural attitudes put in evidence in this Element. Indeed Bonacich and Lu (2012) indicate some open problems that have been tackled by the kinetic theory of active particles and that can be viewed as research perspectives for the mathematical theory of behavioural swarms. In particular, it is mentioned that models should go beyond the consensus dynamics and include heterogeneity of individual behaviors.

The recent literature, as shown in the preceding sections, has tackled these problems within the framework of mathematical tools motivated by statistical physics. The review by Ajmone Marsan et al. (2016) has reported about them. The mathematical theory of behavioural swarms has also taken into account these hints that go beyond the deterministic description. Further steps are discussed in the last chapter of this Element.

7 The Computational Code

This section presents the computational tools, in particular the Python code, that can be used to simulate the price application worthwhile. The reader can find the complete code in a git-like repository.[1]

7.1 Parameters

The parameters shaping the dynamics are the following:

```
#Number of agents in the model
N = 10        #numbers of sellers
M = 50        #numbers of buyers
ratio = M/N  #ratio sellers/buyers
#Parameters for the model
#micro-micro interaction
eta_0 = 1        #intensity of rate of micro-micro interaction
alpha = 1        #intensity of micro-micro interaction for sellers
rho = 2          #intensity of exponential argument in the rate of
                  micro-micro interaction for seller
beta = 0.1       #intensity of micro-micro interaction for buyers
```

[1] https://github.com/Valer7a/Cherry-Picking-in-a-Decentralized-Hayekian-Market-with-Quality-described-through-Swam-Theory/blob/main/Second_Model.ipynb

```
#macro-micro interaction
gamma_s = 0.01  #intensity of macro-micro interaction for sellers
mu_0 = 1        #intensity of rate of macro-micro interaction for sellers
#Number of cycles
n = 50000
```

7.2 The Quantities in the Dynamical System

Here we initialize the arrays containing the quantities (variables in the differential system) defining the dynamics and define their initial conditions, which are necessary for the computational solution of the initial value problem.

```
#PRICES
b = np.full([n,M], 0.0) #buyers prices during time-steps
s = np.full([n,N], 0.0) #sellers prices during time-steps
#VELOCITIES of prices
x = np.full([n,M], 0.0) #buyers prices velocities during time-steps
y = np.full([n,N], 0.0) #sellers prices velocities during time-steps
#MEAN prices
MeanPrice_B = np.full([n,1], 0.0) #buyers mean prices during time-steps
MeanPrice_S = np.full([n,1], 0.0) #sellers mean prices during time-steps
#VARIANCE of prices
VariancePrice_S = np.full([n,1], 0.0) #buyers variance of prices during
                                       time-steps
VariancePrice_B = np.full([n,1], 0.0) #sellers variance of prices during
                                       time-steps
#PARETO MARKET EFFICIENCY
efficiency_S = np.full([n,1], 0.0)   #total buyers efficiency during
                                      time-steps
efficiency_B = np.full([n,1], 0.0)   #total sellers efficiency during
                                      time-steps
efficiency_Tot = np.full([n,1], 0.0) #total market efficiency during
                                      time-steps
#INITIAL CONDITIONS renewed at every time-step (only for the modelling)
z_b0 = [0,0] #initial conditions of every time-step for buyers
z_s0 = [0,0] #initial conditions of every time-step for sellers
#QUALITIES
quality_s = np.full(N, 0.0) #sellers' offered quality
quality_b = np.full(M, 0.0) #buyers' reservation qualities
#SELLERS
#Sellers Initial Cost
s_cost = np.full(N, 0.0)
#BUYERS
#Buyers Chosen Seller at every time step
chosen_seller = np.full([n,M], 0)
#Buyer Chosen Price and Seller renewed at each timestep (only for
 modelling)
b_choices = [0,0]
#SETTING INITIAL CONDITIONS FOR ALL QUANTITIES
#Buyers initial Prices, and Reservation Qualities
```

```
for i in range(0,M):
    #Price
    b[0,i] = random.random()*5 + 1000
    #Quality
    quality_b[i] = random.randint(999,1004)
    print('buyer '+ str(i) + ' quality ' + str(quality_b[i]) )
#to make sure the lowest quality offering seller will have a buyer
quality_b[1] = 999
#Sellers initial Prices, Costs, Qualities
for j in range(0,N):
    #Price
    s[0,j] = random.random()*5 + 1000
    #Cost
    s_cost[j] = (s[0,j])*0.1
    #Quality
    quality_s[j] = random.randint(1000,1005)
    print('seller '+ str(j) + ' quality ' + str(quality_s[j]) )
#to make sure every buyers chooses a seller
quality_s[N-1] = 1005
#Calculation of initial Mean Prices
MeanPrice_S[0] = st.mean(s[0]) #buyers initial mean prices
MeanPrice_B[0] = st.mean(b[0]) #sellers initial mean price
#Calculation of initial Variances of Prices
VariancePrice_S[0] = st.variance(s[0]) #buyers initial variance of prices
VariancePrice_B[0] = st.variance(b[0]) #sellers initial variance of prices
```

In addition, we consider the following functions:

Functions: The functions of the dynamics both for buyers and for sellers. We will have two types of interactions for both agents:

- micro-micro interaction: between the single buyer and the single seller;
- macro-micro interaction: between the single agent and all the FS to which it belongs.

Note that, even if present in the general formulation of the dynamics, we will not consider the interaction among buyers.

Buyers: Functions defining buyers' prices adaptation (through interaction).

```
#BUYERS FUNCTIONS
#Micro-Micro
#Function defining rate of micro-micro interaction
def eta_b(bb,ss,ratio,eta_0):
    if -0.01 < bb < 0.01:
        argument = (np.abs((ss-bb)/0.01))
    else:
        argument = (np.abs((ss-bb)/bb))
    xx = -(ratio)*(argument)
    etab = eta_0 * (np.exp(xx))
    return etab
```

```
#Function defining micro-micro interaction
def fi_b(bb,ss,beta):
    fib = beta * (ss-bb)
    return fib
#Function defining the seller with which the buyer will interact
def choice(s,quality_b,quality_s):
    acc_s = [] #stands for acceptable sellers, the sellers with quality
                high enough for the buyer
    l = 0 #to count which are acceptable sellers
    for m in range(0,N):
        if quality_s[m] >= quality_b:
            acc_s.append(m) #registering all sellers with the right
                             quality
            l = l + 1
    chosen_price = s[acc_s[0]]
    b_choice = acc_s[0]
    for j in range(0,l-1): #choosing the seller with the lowest price
                            among the acceptable ones
            if (chosen_price > s[acc_s[j+1]]):
                chosen_price = s[acc_s[j+1]]
                b_choice = acc_s[j+1]
            elif (chosen_price == s[acc_s[j+1]]):
                chosen_price = s[acc_s[j]]
                b_choice = random.choice([s[acc_s[j]], s[acc_s[j+1]]])
    #returns price of the chosen seller and the chosen seller in this
    order return chosen_price,b_choice
#Whole Dynamics
#Function defining the whole dynamics of buyers' acceleration in ODE
def model_b(z_b,_,min_price,ratio,beta,N,eta_0):
    b = z_b[0]
    x = z_b[1]
    sumx = (eta_b(b,min_price,ratio,eta_0)) * fi_b(b,min_price,beta)
    dbdt = x
    dxdt = (1/N) * sumx
    return [dbdt,dxdt]
```

Sellers: Functions defining sellers' prices adaptation (through interaction).

```
#SELLERS FUNCTIONS
#Micro-Micro
#Function defining rate of micro-micro interaction
def eta_s(s,ratio,eta_0,rho):
    xx = -(rho/ratio)*np.abs(s)
    etas = eta_0 * (np.exp(xx))
    return etas
#Function defining micro-micro interaction
def fi_s(b,s,alpha,chosen_s,s_counter):
    if (chosen_s == s_counter): #here seller knows if it is the chosen
                                 seller for buyer i
        if (b<s):
            sig = -1
        else:
            sig = 1
```

```
    else:
        sig = -1
    fis = alpha*np.abs(s)*sig
    return fis
#Macro-Micro
#Function defining macro-micro interaction
def psi_s(s,E1,gamma_s):
    psis = gamma_s*(E1 - s)
    return psis
#Whole Dynamics
#Function defining the whole dynamics of sellers' acceleration in ODE
def model_s(z_s,_,b,E1,mu_0,eta_0,alpha,M,gamma_s,chosen_s,s_counter,rho):
    s = z_s[0]
    y = z_s[1]
    sumy = 0.0 #sum on buyers (interaction of the seller j with all
                buyers)
    for i in range(0,M):
        sumy = sumy + (eta_s(s,ratio,eta_0,rho)*fi_s(b[i],s,alpha,
        chosen_s[i],s_counter))
    dsdt = y
    dydt = (1/M)*(sumy) + mu_0 * psi_s(s,E1,gamma_s)
    return [dsdt,dydt]
```

7.3 Some Technical Considerations

As mentioned earlier, we have reported the Python code to obtain the simulation associated with the class of models proposed in Section 4. This type of programming is quite standard, but it considers the possibility of a sensitivity analysis of the parameters, so that the user can develop a study of the whole variety of predictions that can be delivered by the model; in particular, the different types of aggregations that the system seller-buyer exhibits. Indeed, the simulations in Section 4 have shown this specific feature of the dynamics.

Referring to the contents of Section 5, we can deduce that the same dynamics can be described by the kinetic theory of active particles with discrete states. Furthermore, one can develop models where behavioural swarms are used for sellers, while kinetic theory is used for buyers. The derivation of new codes to consider this evolution of models follows techniques close to those we have presented in this section. The interested reader should develop them autonomously thanks to the hints given in this section.

8 Closure: On the Role of Hard Sciences in Economic Theories

This Element has shown how mathematical sciences can contribute to formalize behavioural economic theories in a rigorous mathematical framework. In particular, two different theories have been examined and related to specific applications. The Element has also proposed further developments of the previously mentioned theories according to the motivations generated by specific applications.

This conclusive section provides some free considerations about the so-called soft and hard sciences. Actually, this classification of *hard sciences* and *soft sciences* was proposed by August Compte (2012, 1839) also as an answer to a dispute in which physics and chemistry were considered sciences, while the others were not sciences. In this framework physics and chemistry are supported by theories, while the others could only rely on experiments.

We do not agree with this drastic interpretation; rather we think that all sciences should develop a quest toward a theory. Indeed, we agree with Diamond (1987) that

> ***Soft sciences are harder than hard sciences.***

Before proceeding with these speculations, we should mention that experiments are, however, important to validate theories. Otherwise, if not related to a theory, the validity is limited to *hic et nunc*. In the case of behavioral economics the experiment should also consider that living matter evolves over time. In the case of *behavioural economics*, the interaction of economics is with what has been called *science of living systems*; see Bellomo et al. (2017). This Element contributes to the understanding of how this complex interaction can be developed.

- **Q1. Why is behavioural economics a very difficult guest for mathematics?**
  The difficulties have been well explained in the previous sections. In fact, behaviours are those of living systems. Mathematics must then operate within the general framework of the science of living systems. In this framework, individual interactions can be transferred to describe the collective dynamics by the kinetic theory of active particles. However, the rules of interaction evolve over time within the artificial world.
  The preceding characteristics require advanced studies, which have only recently produced satisfactory results. An additional problem is the presence of ideological components that are always present in economics. It is a stone guest that creates additional difficulties.
- **Q2. What is the role of mathematics in its interaction with economics?**
  Mathematics is supposed to translate the conceptual framework of economic theories into differential systems with the ability to provide a wide variety of predictions, as shown in the application presented in Section 4. The present Element suggests that modelling should not be approached by each case study through a stand-alone approach.

On the other hand, the Element proposes to derive a general theory that is valid for a wide variety of applications, so that specific case studies can be dealt with by specializing such a theory.

- **Q3. What is the advantage that mathematics can bring to economics?**
  Mathematics' support for economics, as important as it is, is not only technical, as the answers to the first two questions show. In fact, mathematics can explore global aspects of the description of the dynamics of economic systems and can address challenging objectives such as events that are difficult to predict, such as the so-called black swan. Accordingly, we can say that mathematics can refine and even improve economic theories, to the point of becoming part of them.
- **Q4. What is the benefit that economics can bring to mathematics?**
  Given a theory and specific problems in economics, the contribution of mathematics cannot be delivered by a straightforward transfer of known tools. In most cases, such a contribution requires the invention of new tools and even new theories.
  When this happens, it is a sunny day for mathematicians.
- **Q5. How far are we from a mathematical theory of economics?**
  We are pleased to note that some advances have already characterized the field of research under consideration. Some of them have been reported and critically analyzed in this Element. What comes next?
  Economic theories evolve over time to follow the changes in our society. Mathematics can then follow this evolution and develop new mathematical theories. This is also what happens in other sciences within a global vision, where progress requires an interdisciplinary vision. Then all the sciences involved in the preceding discussion are continuously progressing, and this story has not ended.

References

Aguiar, M., Dosi, G., Knopoff, D. A., & Virgillito, M. E. (2021). A multi-scale network-based model of contagion dynamics: Heterogeneity, spatial distancing and vaccination. *Mathematical Models and Methods in Applied Sciences*, *31*, 2425–2454.

Ajmone Marsan, G., Bellomo, N., & Gibelli, L. (2016). Stochastic evolutionary differential games toward a systems theory of behavioral social dynamics. *Mathematical Models and Methods in Applied Sciences*, *26*(06), 1051–1093.

Anderson, P. W. (1972). More is different. *Science*, *177*(4047), 393–396.

Aristov, V. (2019). Biological systems as nonequilibrium structures described by kinetic methods. *Results in Physics*, *13*, 102232.

Bae, H.-O., Cho, S.-Y., Kim, J., & Yun, S.-B. (2019). A kinetic description for the herding behavior in financial market. *Journal of Statistical Physics*, *176*, 398–424.

Bae, H.-O., Cho, S.-Y., Lee, S.-H., Yoo, J., & Yun, S.-B. (2019). A particle model for the herding phenomena induced by dynamic market signals. *Journal of Statistical Physics*, *177*, 365–398.

Ball, P. (2012). *Why society is a complex matter*. Springer Science & Business Media.

Bandura, A. (1989). Human agency in social cognitive theory. *American Psychologist*, *44*(9), 1175–1184.

Bellomo, N. (2008). *Living systems*. Birkhäuser-Springer.

Bellomo, N., Bellouquid, A., Gibelli, L., & Outada, N. (2017). *A quest towards a mathematical theory of living systems*. Birkhäuser-Springer.

Bellomo, N., Burini, D., Dosi, G., Gibelli, L., Knopoff, D., Outada, N., Terna, P., and Virgillito, M. E. (2021). What is life? A perspective of the mathematical kinetic theory of active particles. *Mathematical Models and Methods in Applied Sciences*, *31*(09), 1821–1866.

Bellomo, N., & Carbonaro, B. (2011). Toward a mathematical theory of living systems focusing on developmental biology and evolution: A review and perspectives. *Physics of Life Reviews*, *8*(1), 1–18.

Bellomo, N., Colasuonno, F., Knopoff, D., & Soler, J. (2015). From a systems theory of sociology to modeling the onset and evolution of criminality. *Networks and Heterogeneous Media*, *10*, 421–441.

Bellomo, N., De Nigris, S., Knopoff, D., Morini, M., & Terna, P. (2020). Swarms dynamics towards a systems approach to social sciences and behavioral economy. *Networks and Heterogeneous Media*, *15*, 353–368.

Bellomo, N., Dosi, G., Knopoff, D. A., & Virgillito, M. E. (2020). From particles to firms: On the kinetic theory of climbing up evolutionary landscapes. *Mathematical Models and Methods in Applied Sciences*, *30*(07), 1441–1460.

Bellomo, N., & Egidi, M. (2024). From Herbert A. Simon's legacy to the evolutionary artificial world with heterogeneous collective behaviorss. *Mathematical Models and Methods in Applied Sciences*, *34*(1), 145–180. https://doi.org/10.1142/S0218202524400049.

Bellomo, N., Esfahanian, M., Secchini, V., & Terna, P. (2022). What is life? Active particles tools towards behavioral dynamics in social-biology and economics. *Physics of Life Reviews*, *43*, 189–207.

Bellomo, N., & Forni, G. (1994). Dynamics of tumor interaction with the host immune system. *Mathematical and Computer Modelling*, *20*(1), 107–122.

Bellomo, N., Ha, S.-Y., & Outada, N. (2020). Towards a mathematical theory of behavioral swarms. *ESAIM: Control, Optimisation and Calculus of Variations*, *26*, 125.

Bellomo, N., Herrero, M. A., & Tosin, A. (2013). On the dynamics of social conflicts looking for the Black Swan. *Kinetic Related Models*, *6*(3), 459–479.

Bellouquid, A., & Delitala, M. (2006). *Modelling complex biological systems: A kinetic theory approach*. Birkhäuser-Springer.

Bertotti, M. L. (2010). Modelling taxation and redistribution: A discrete active particle kinetic approach. *Applied Mathematics and Computation*, *217*(2), 752–762.

Bertotti, M. L., & Delitala, M. (2004). From discrete kinetic and stochastic game theory to modelling complex systems in applied sciences. *Mathematical Models and Methods in Applied Sciences*, *14*(07), 1061–1084.

Bertotti, M. L., & Delitala, M. (2010). Cluster formation in opinion dynamics: A qualitative analysis. *Zeitschrift für angewandte Mathematik und Physik*, *61*, 583–602.

Bertotti, M. L., & Modanese, G. (2011). From microscopic taxation and redistribution models to macroscopic income distributions. *Physica A: Statistical Mechanics and Its Applications*, *390*(21–22), 3782–3793.

Black, F., & Scholes, M. (1972). The valuation of option contracts and a test of market efficiency. *The Journal of Finance*, *27*(2), 399–417.

Black, F., & Scholes, M. (1973). The pricing of options and corporate liabilities. *Journal of Political Economy*, *81*(3), 637–654.

Bonacich, P., & Lu, P. (2012). *Introduction to mathematical sociology*. Princeton University Press.

Burini, D., & Chouhad, N. (2022). Virus models in complex frameworks: Towards modeling space patterns of SARS-CoV-2 epidemics. *Mathematical Models and Methods in Applied Sciences*, *32*(10), 2017–2036.

Burini, D., & Chouhad, N. (2023). Cross diffusion models in complex frameworks from microscopic to macroscopic. *Mathematical Models and Methods in Applied Sciences*, *33*(9), 158–162.

Burini, D., Chouhad, N., & Bellomo, N. (2023). Waiting for a mathematical theory of living systems from a critical review to research perspectives. *Symmetry*, *15*(2), 351.

Burini, D., & De Lillo, S. (2019). On the complex interaction between collective learning and social dynamics. *Symmetry*, *11*(8), 967.

Burini, D., De Lillo, S., & Gibelli, L. (2016). Collective learning modeling based on the kinetic theory of active particles. *Physics of Life Reviews*, *16*, 123–139.

Burini, D., Gibelli, L., & Outada, N. (2017). A kinetic theory approach to the modeling of complex living systems. *Active Particles*, *1*, 229–258.

Burini, D., & Knopoff, D. A. (2024). Epidemics and society: A multiscale vision from the *Small World* to the *Globally Interconnected World*. *Mathematical Models and Methods in Applied Sciences*, *34*(08), 1567–1596.

Compte, A. (2012, 1839). *Cours de philosophie positive*. Hermann.

Coscia, V., Delitala, M., & Frasca, P. (2007). On the mathematical theory of vehicular traffic flow models II. Discrete velocity kinetic models. *International Journal of Non-Linear Mechanics*, *42*(3), 411–421.

Cucker, F., & Smale, S. (2007). Emergent behavior in flocks. *IEEE Transactions on Automatic Control*, *52*(5), 852–862.

Diamond, J. (1987). Soft sciences are often harder than hard sciences. *Discover*, *8*(8), 34–39.

Dolfin, M., Knopoff, D., Leonida, L., & Patti, D. M. A. (2017). Escaping the trap of "blocking": A kinetic model linking economic development and political competition. *Kinetic and Related Models*, *24*, 2361–2381.

Dolfin, M., & Lachowicz, M. (2014). Modeling altruism and selfishness in welfare dynamics: The role of nonlinear interactions. *Mathematical Models and Methods in Applied Sciences*, *24*(12), 2361–2381.

Dolfin, M., & Lachowicz, M. (2015). Modeling opinion dynamics: How the network enhances consensus. *Networks and Heterogeneous Media*, *10*(4), 877–896.

Dolfin, M., Leonida, L., & Outada, N. (2017). Modeling human behavior in economics and social science. *Physics of Life Reviews*, *22*, 1–21.

Dosi, G. (1984). Technology and conditions of macroeconomic development. In C. Freeman (Ed.), *Design, innovation and long cycles in economic development* (pp. 99–125). Design Research Publications.

Dosi, G. (2023). *The foundations of complex evolving economies: Part one: Innovation, organization, and industrial dynamics*. Oxford University Press.

Dosi, G., Fanti, L., & Virgillito, M. E. (2020). Unequal societies in usual times, unjust societies in pandemic ones. *Journal of Industrial and Business Economics*, *47*, 371–389.

Dosi, G., Pereira, M. C., & Virgillito, M. E. (2017). The footprint of evolutionary processes of learning and selection upon the statistical properties of industrial dynamics. *Industrial and Corporate Change*, *26*(2), 187–210.

Dosi, G., & Virgillito, M. E. (2021). In order to stand up you must keep cycling: Change and coordination in complex evolving economies. *Structural Change and Economic Dynamics*, *56*, 353–364.

Furioli, G., Pulvirenti, A., Terraneo, E., & Toscani, G. (2017). Fokker–Planck equations in the modeling of socio-economic phenomena. *Mathematical Models and Methods in Applied Sciences*, *27*(01), 115–158.

Galam, S. (2012). *Sociophysics: A physicist's modeling of psycho-political phenomena (understanding complex systems)*. Berlin: Springer.

Ha, S.-Y., Kim, J., Park, J., & Zhang, X. (2019). Complete cluster predictability of the Cucker–Smale flocking model on the real line. *Archive for Rational Mechanics and Analysis*, *231*, 319–365.

Hartwell, L. H., Hopfield, J. J., Leibler, S., & Murray, A. W. (1999). From molecular to modular cell biology. *Nature*, *402*(Suppl 6761), C47–C52.

Helbing, D. (2010). *Quantitative sociodynamics: Stochastic methods and models of social interaction processes*. Springer Science & Business Media.

Hilbert, D. (1902). Mathematical problems. *Bulletin American Mathematical Society*, *8*, 437–479.

Jager, E., & Segel, L. A. (1992). On the distribution of dominance in populations of social organisms. *SIAM Journal on Applied Mathematics*, *52*(5), 1442–1468.

Jovanovic, F., & Le Gall, P. (2021). Mathematical analogies: An engine for understanding the transfers between economics and physics. *History of Economics Review*, *79*(1), 18–38.

Kant, I. (2000). *Critique of the power of judgment*. Cambridge University Press.

Knopoff, D. (2014). On a mathematical theory of complex systems on networks with application to opinion formation. *Mathematical Models and Methods Applied Sciences*, *24*(405–426).

Knopoff, D., Secchini, V., & Terna, P. (2020). Cherry picking: Consumer choices in swarm dynamics, considering price and quality of goods. *Symmetry*, *12*(11), 1912.

Lachowicz, M., Matusik, M., & Topolski, K. A. (2024). Population of entities with three individual states and asymmetric interactions. *Applied Mathematics and Computation*, *464*.

May, R. M. (2004). Uses and abuses of mathematics in biology. *Science, 303*(5659), 790–793.

Mayr, E. (1981). *La biologie de l'évolution*. Paris: Hermann.

Mazzoli, M., Morini, M., & Terna, P. (2019). *Rethinking macroeconomics with endogenous market structure*. Cambridge University Press.

Nash, J. (1951). Non-cooperative games. *Annals of Mathematics*, 286–295.

Nash, J. (1996). *Essays on game theory*. Cheltenham, UK: Elgar.

Pareschi, L., & Toscani, G. (2013). *Interacting multiagent systems: Kinetic equations and Monte Carlo methods*. Oxford: Oxford University Press.

Paveri-Fontana, S. L. (1975). On Boltzmann-like treatments for traffic flow. *Transportation Research, 9*(4), 225–235.

Perlovsky, L., & Schoeller, F. (2019). Unconscious emotions of human learning. *Physics of Life Reviews, 31*, 257–262.

Prigogine, I., & Herman, R. (1971). *Kinetic theory of vehicular traffic*. New York: Elsevier.

Reed, M. C. (2004). Why is mathematical biology so hard. *Notices of the AMS, 51*(3), 338–342.

Salomon, G., & Perkins, D. N. (1998). Individual and social aspects of learning. *Review of Research in Education, 23*(1), 1–24.

Schoeller, F., Perlovsky, L., & Arseniev, D. (2018). Physics of mind: Experimental confirmations of theoretical predictions. *Physics of Life Reviews, 25*, 45–68.

Schumpeter, J. A. (1947). *Capitalism, socialism and democracy*. Taylor and Francis.

Simon, H. A. (1978). Rational decision making in business organizations. *Nobel Memorial Lecture, 8 December, 69*(4), 493–513. Retrieved from www.nobelprize.org/uploads/2018/06/simon-lecture.pdf

Simon, H. A. (2019). *The sciences of the artificial, third edition*. Massachusetts Institute of Technology Press.

Stiglitz, J. E. (2010). *Freefall: America, free markets, and the sinking of the world economy*. W. W. Norton & Company.

Taleb, N. N. (2007). *The black swan: The impact of the highly improbable*. Random house.

Thaler, R. H. (2016). Behavioral economics: Past, present, and future. *American Economic Review, 106*(7), 1577–1600.

Thaler, R. H., & Sunstein, C. R. (2009). *Nudge: Improving decisions about health, wealth, and happiness*. Penguin.

Zhang, W.-B. (1991). *Synergetic economics*. Heidelberg: Springer.

Zhang, W.-B. (2023). *Chaos, complexity, and nonlinear economic theory*. Singapore, London: World Scientific.

Acknowledgements

Nicola Bellomo acknowledges the partial support by Grant PID2022-1372 28OB-I00 funded by the Spanish Ministerio de Ciencia, Innovación y Universidades, MICIU/AEI/10.13039/501100011033 & 'ERDF/EU A way of making Europe,' by Grant C-EXP-265-UGR23 funded by Consejería de Universidad, Investigación e Innovación & ERDF/EU Andalusia Program, and by Modeling Nature Research Unit, project QUAL21-011.

Valeria Secchini acknowledges the support from the Czech Science Foundation (CORPTAX, 21-05547M), the Cooperation Program at Charles University, research area Economics, and the Charles University Grant Agency (GAUK, 254322).

All authors thank the referees whose remarks have definitely contributed to improve the quality of the presentation of the contents of our Element.

Cambridge Elements ☰

Complexity and Agent-Based Economics

Giovanni Dosi

Sant'Anna School of Advanced Studies

Giovanni Dosi is Professor Emeritus of Economics at Sant'Anna School of Advanced Studies, Pisa (Italy) and Editor for the Americas of the journal *Industrial and Corporate Change*. He is included in the ISI Highly Cited Research list, denoting those who made fundamental contributions to the advancement of science and technology, and is a corresponding member of the Accademia Nazionale dei Lincei, the first academy of sciences in Italy. He received, in 2016, the Wiley TIM Distinguished Scholar Award by the Technology and Innovation Management Division of the American Academy of Management, in 2022 the Penrose Prize of the European Academy of Management, and, in 2024, the Schumpeter Prize. His major research areas – where he is author and editor of several works – include Economics of Innovation and Technological Change, Industrial Economics, Evolutionary Theory, Economic Growth and Development, Organizational Studies.

Mauro Gallegati

Università Politecnica delle Marche

Mauro Gallegati is full Professor of Advanced Economics at the Università Politecnica delle Marche, Ancona, Italy. His research concerns interdisciplinary applications of complex systems with heterogeneous interacting agents and econophysics. He is one of the pioneers of agent-based models and economic complexity. He published several papers and books. His methods of asymmetric information settings are widely used by academicians. His research interests range from ABM economics to economic history, to mathematics, to complexity and networks.

Simone Landini

IRES Piemonte

Simone Landini is Senior Researcher at the Socioeconomic Research Institute of Piedmont (IRES Piemonte), Turin, Italy. He holds a PhD in Mathematics for the Analysis of Financial Markets, had been awarded the INET Grant and had been a Visiting Fellow in the University of Technology of Sydney. His research interests include applied mathematics, quantitative methods for economics, finance, regional and social sciences, agent-based modelling and computability theory. He published articles in international peer-reviewed journals.

Maria Enrica Virgillito
Sant'Anna School of Advanced Studies

Maria Enrica Virgillito is Associate Professor in Economics at the Institute of Economics, Sant'Anna School of Advanced Studies, Pisa, Italy where she coordinates the Seasonal School in "Agent-Based models in Economics". Her publications have been hosted in a number of international scientific peer-reviewed journals in the realms of complexity economics, institutional labour economics, evolutionary economics. She is Global Labour Organization Fellow and serves as Editor for the Macro and Development yearly issue of Industrial and Corporate Change, as Associate Editor for Structural Change and Economic Dynamics and for the Review of Evolutionary Political Economy.

About the Series

Elements in Complexity and Agent-Based Economics will present the state-of-the-art in complexity and agent-based economics with the aim of offering a systematic and easy-to-access thematic organization of both consolidated results, and the latest developments in the fields. Contributions are meant both as a support to scholarly research and as teaching tools.

Cambridge Elements

Complexity and Agent-Based Economics

Elements in the Series

Active Particles Methods in Economics: New Perspectives in the Interaction between Mathematics and Economics
Nicola Bellomo, Diletta Burini, Valeria Secchini and Pietro Terna

A full series listing is available at: www.cambridge.org/ECAE

For EU product safety concerns, contact us at Calle de José Abascal, 56–1°, 28003 Madrid, Spain or eugpsr@cambridge.org.

www.ingramcontent.com/pod-product-compliance
Ingram Content Group UK Ltd.
Pitfield, Milton Keynes, MK11 3LW, UK
UKHW022143080726
473066UK00010B/721

* 9 7 8 1 0 0 9 5 4 8 7 6 2 *